REDISTRIBUTING POWER IN THE COUNSELOR-CLIENT RELATIONSHIP

PARTNERS IN HEALING

BY BARBARA FRIEDMAN, Ph.D.

Resource Publications, Inc.
San Jose, California

Editorial director: Kenneth Guentert
Managing editor: Elizabeth J. Asborno
Cover production: Huey Lee
Cover illustration: Barbara Friedman
Copyeditor: Dianne Braden

Reprint Department
Resource Publications, Inc.
160 E. Virginia Street #290
San Jose, CA 95112-5876

Library of Congress Cataloging in Publication Data
Friedman, Barbara, 1945-
    Partners in healing : redistributing power in the
counselor-client relationship / by Barbara Friedman.
        p.   cm.
    Includes bibliographical references and index.
    ISBN 0-89390-226- 8
    1. Counselor and client. 2. Psychotherapist and
patient. 3. Feminist theory. 4. Control (Psychology)
I. Title.
    BF637.C6F687   1992
    158'.3 — dc20   92-3111

96 95 94 93 92 | 5 4 3 2 1

Contents

Acknowledgments

First and foremost I am indebted to my clients for the honor of their trust and the privilege of their company in the dance of therapy.

My gratitude to and appreciation for the efforts of my editor, friend and co-conspirator, Dianne Braden, cannot be adequately expressed. It was largely through our interaction that I developed the understanding of relationship which I describe in this book. With her support I grew strong enough and clear enough to write.

I also want to give special acknowledgment to those writers whose careful research and inspired thinking provided the philosophical structure with which I have supported my ideas. Each of them is an advanced thinker in their field, blending a feminine and masculine consciousness. Each of them discarded the old rigid rules for a more fluid and flexible model. Dr. Vocatta George provided me with a thorough history of the Goddess in western civilization and with an understanding of the evolutionary relationship humankind has with the deity. Evelyn Fox Keller's gift to me was her expressive genius in explaining the effects of gender on science. Lastly I would like to thank Gary Zukov, whose work helped me to understand and explain quantum physics. When I read his work I knew his views were true for therapy as well.

My deepest appreciation goes to my family: to Anna for her grounding, to my son Devin and my daughter Promise for growing with me, to my husband Angelo for his unwavering support, and to my daughter Michelle who has always been there for me. Finally I am indebted to Bryan Christopher for his vision.

Introduction

Change is not meaningless—if it were there
would be no knowledge of it.[1]

The therapeutic relationship, as it is classically defined, is often diametrically opposed to the kind of healing needed in our times. Counselors today must nurture the growth of personal power and relationship. The traditional distant and authoritarian stance is incompatible with that goal.

One client described it this way.

> I sat across the table from my second therapist, wondering how she could look so together and I could be such a mess, *again!* I just kept wondering how long I would stay this time; how much longer I could tolerate feeling like the screw-up I knew I was. Why else would I be there? Part of me hoped to God she had the answers she was supposed to have as a therapist; hoping it didn't show how much I wanted someone to have the answers for me. The other part of me was just plain scared; scared that I would have laid myself bare to one more stranger who would listen and then tell me how serious my problems seemed from their lofty and safe perspective. I was suddenly struck in the pit of my stomach by that sickeningly familiar recognition; the one that reminds me I'm defective and need to be fixed. Dreading what I knew I would hear, I held my breath like a child

waiting for the punishment that was sure to follow her crime.

The old definition of the therapeutic relationship keeps the client and therapist locked in a deadly embrace. The client whispers into the therapist's ear, "You know. Please tell me." And the therapist responds with soft advice. The price for the client is high: dependency and an illusionary world without personal power or responsibility. The price for the therapist is just as high: living in a fantasy world built on inflation. There is a higher price still, for both of them: the limitation of healing through relationship.

From my personal experience as both a client and a therapist, I know it is easy to be seduced into believing I have the answers and just as easy to be seduced into believing that someone else does. Because I have been on both sides, it should be obvious to me that neither is true. Yet time and again when I sit on one side, I assume omnipotence, and on the other side, I project it.

But who is doing the seducing? It is that old vampire power, seducing the client and counselor with the sweet words they want so much to believe, taking advantage of their fear, seeking their most vulnerable spots. To the client it says, "Someone has the answers. Now you can finally be safe." Then taking a second, almost imperceptible bite, it says to the counselor, "And it is you who has them." When either of them resists, the vampire frightens them by asking, "If the counselor doesn't have the answers, then who does?" Panic sets in. "Someone must have the answers," they both agree. So in their desperation, they want to believe the vampire; they offer up their necks against their better judgment.

Throughout the world today, peoples' eyes are opening to the effects of the abuse of power. We are now well aware that a relationship where one person has power over another is abusive. We see the consequences all around us on both a cultural and personal level. We wage war and name the shadow side of our world "psyche," the evil psychotic enemy. We build up armaments to protect ourselves and remain surprised that an abused people would become crazed with rage. We separate ourselves, and it becomes "me versus them." We relate as an "I" to an "It." From this objectified distance, we can kill for peace.

We have uncovered the devastating fact that the abuse of power is widespread in our own society as well. It is sadly commonplace. The distance between "me and them" is growing smaller. Feminists and people recovering from the ravages of alcohol and drug addiction took up the lead in the creation of an atmosphere where abuse victims could speak without shame. A tremendous number of abused women, children, and most recently men, have come forward to tell their stories. When they do, we discover they are members of our own families.

Because of the epidemic proportions of this problem, social science researchers are spending much of their time studying abuse—its causes and effects. Their results indicate that abuse occurs when one person has power over another, objectifies the other, and projects their own unwanted qualities onto the other. The ramifications for both the victim and the perpetrator are profound, leaving lifelong devastation. And the effects don't stop there. They are passed on through generations, a legacy of depression and self-perpetuating imbalance.

When we are the helping professionals working with this devastation every day, the distance between me and them is difficult to maintain. When we see women and men struggling for intimacy in their lives: addicted to drugs, food, or sex; living at a sufferance in isolation; or acting out their rage with violence, we understand the trauma abuse causes: the ravaged lives.

When we are the clients uncovering from our own well-defended memories the time when we were part of an abusive relationship, the distance disappears completely. In our most open and integrated moments, we realize within ourselves both the abuser and the abused. In the final merging, we step away from any separation at all. We own how we are abusive to ourselves within our own personal psyche. We recognize our own degrading voice saying to ourselves, "You're stupid, fat, and unlovable!" Finally we become aware of our self-abuse.

So we as therapists and clients are in a predicament. History hands down to us a pre-structured relationship. State laws governing psychologists exemplifies the structure we are given.

> The board finds that the effects of the psychologist-client relationship are powerful and subtle and that clients are influenced consciously and subconsciously by the *unequal distribution of power in such relationships.*[2]

Think carefully about what these laws are actually saying. They state that it is inherent to the therapeutic relationship that the client is less powerful than the therapist, that a dominant/subordinate relationship exists. And as a society, we accept this unequal distribution of power as an unquestionable fact, a given. At the same time, we know that a relationship based on this type of power dynamic is destructive.

We have set up a relationship of dominance and subordination which inevitably produces a power struggle with all of its harmful ramifications. Is it healing to be in either position—inferior or superior, infantilized or inflated? This scenario has the dangerous potential to inflict the very wound helping professionals are trying to heal.

We as a society definitely sense that something about the relationship feels wrong, and we scramble to make it right. We know that in the relationship as it exists, the client is at risk of being abused. In an humanitarian effort to protect clients, whom we see as defenseless, from the adverse effects of this unequal distribution of power, we create laws to regulate the relationship and ethics committees to police it. We hope that the threat of public shaming, loss of income and social status will keep therapists in line. But these external threats just place therapists in the victim role. It prohibits them from owning their own power.

The very existence of these laws implies society already understands the destructive nature of the relationship as it exists. We are aware that corruption and exploitation result from this kind of power dynamic. And we are right to try to safeguard clients from this. Yet we never see, let alone question, the basic assumption that creates all of these problems and many more— the assumption that there must be an "unequal distribution of power" in the therapeutic relationship.

When clients ask their counselors, "Why such rigid rules?" their counselors do a quick theoretical shuffle from their stance of empowerment. With authoritative assurance, they tell their clients, "Most dysfunctions today are really boundary confusions caused by unclear role definitions in the family of origin." Counselors assure their clients they keep their rigid boundaries for their clients' protection, telling them, "People with boundary confusion do not have the common sense needed to set limits and form identity and relationship boundaries."[3] Counselors take it upon themselves to do this for their clients.

Why does society take this power disparity as a given? Because it is as normal as the relationship between parent and child, student and teacher, employer and employee, doctor and patient. It is so normal that we are oblivious to the possibility that any of these relationships could be structured in any other way. The therapeutic relationship simply mirrors the structure of other relationships in our culture.

Therapists have such good intentions, but something is profoundly wrong with the picture. The client faces the therapist believing the therapist knows what's best. Through this kind of relationship, the therapist then expects the client to feel whole and powerful and able to reclaim control over life.

On one level, often just beneath consciousness, both client and therapist are well aware of the contradiction. They understand that safety is essential to a healing relationship. But a blind spot prevents them from discovering why the relationship, as it is, does not provide this safety. This limits how healing the relationship can actually be. As long as both parties perceive the therapist as powerful and the client as helpless, they prevent healing and growth.

A redistribution of power is necessary in order for the therapeutic relationship to be safe and healing in our times. Therapists and clients need a relationship which supports each of their personal power. In this new relationship, there will be an exchange based on mutual respect. Decisions will be made in reciprocity. The therapist and client will be partners in healing.

I.
HISTORY

This world of the immutable is the demoniac
world, in which there is no free choice, in
which everything is fixed. It is the world of
yin. But in addition to this rigid world of
number, there are living trends. These
develop, consolidate in a given direction,
grow rigid, then decline; a change sets in,
coherence is maintained. He who succeeds in
endowing his work with this regenerative
power creates something organic, and the
thing so created is enduring.[1]

How did clients and therapists get into this predicament? They find themselves tightly bound by a series of tangled contradictions, unable to find the thread to unravel them. An answer to this question lies in looking at the history of relationship. Using a wide-angle lens to view it, we see that the history of relationship follows a clear progression. From this perspective we can begin to see how the uneven distribution of power in the therapeutic relationship emerged and was then progressively and completely folded out of sight under the cloak of normalcy. This historical view depicts the present disequilibrium in the therapeutic relationship as a developmental stage. Society is in a dynamic period of transition, foreshadowing a shift to a deeper understanding of connection.

The dynamics of the therapeutic relationship can only be grasped in a cultural context. Therapy happens between people at a particular time and place in history. Its nature and parameters mirror cultural expectations. Picture Dr. Freud's consulting room. There he sits, his legs crossed, hands folded. His patient, Dora, lies quietly, her right arm limply falling over the side of the couch, the back of her left hand resting lightly on her forehead.[2] She confesses; he listens and analyzes. This scene certainly reflects a Victorian relationship in structure and definition. Contrast this with another cross-legged bearded therapist. This time it's 1972 at Eslin Institute in Big Sur, California. Both client and therapist sit on pillows, facing each other. The therapist quietly chants an internal "Om" while the client focuses on "tuning in." In just this seventy-year period, we can see how the nature of the therapeutic relationship changed.

Let's look back over history in order to gain a better understanding of how this relationship changed over time. When humans began their existence as a species on earth, they were not conscious of themselves. They did not think of themselves as individual entities, separate from nature, a deity, or each other. They lived instinctively and spontaneously. In relationship to the Deity and nature, the "I" and the "Thou" were one.[3] Our early ancestors did not rock back on their prehistoric heels and reflect, "Oh wow! We're in the one." They were a part of existence without knowledge of being a part.

"Out of this state of unitary reality...characterized by the relative absence of any differentiation between subject and environment,"[4] people began to form their first tentative identity. As the historical process unfolded, they gradually became more "self" conscious. It was as if they had been traveling in a dense fog and suddenly came upon a clearing. As they stepped into the open, they suddenly saw themselves as small and extremely vulnerable. The dawning of Self-consciousness may not have been an "a-ha" experience. It was probably more like an "Oh, no!" The more aware people became of themselves, the better they assessed their position. They recognized quickly that they were totally dependent on Mother Nature, an awesome and seemingly arbitrary power. They were at her mercy. She could be generous, graciously providing for all their needs from her bounty. Then suddenly she could burn with hot anger or icy rage, threatening their very lives.

When humans found they were separate from nature, they gave her a feminine form and deified her as the Goddess. They related to her with a mixture of love and fear. They venerated her and sought to appease her. They wanted to be synchronized with her and devoted themselves to her with religious fervor. Worship of the Goddess was widespread in early history, reaching across Europe, Crete, Greece, Egypt, and all of Asia Minor. People in different cultures referred to her by different names: in Sumeria as Ishtar, in Syria as Astarte, in Egypt as Isis, and according to the Old Testament, in Babylonia as Ashtoreth and Anath. But in all of her forms or symbolic identities, the female deity filled the same need: through her, people sought the ecstasy of reconnection and relief from their separateness.

Although the Goddess represented wholeness and oneness, her very existence bespoke separation. From the distance created by this separation, humanity entered its first conscious relationship filled with anxiety, hope, and excited expectation. Their experience was like a child's with its mother. The relationship was at first truly erotic: synthesis, quintessential relatedness. Later it was transfigured by historical developments, its alluring eroticism smothered with dark incestuous anxiety. In time humankind was left with only the euphoric recall of that initial relationship.

People did not restrict the Goddess they worshiped to one symbolic form. When they prayed to her as matriarch, creatrix, fertilizer of the faithful, they idolized her body as the source. They depicted her vagina as a cornucopia spilling forth its bounty. In "On the Moon and Matriarchal Consciousness,"[5] Erich Neuman tells us that she also took the form of Moon Goddess. Then people honored her tidal quality, her ebbing and flowing with the constant, rhythmical changes of eternity. Worshipers followed her into a time that was not linear, not parceled out in minutes — rather, one that moved gradually, like the shifting of the seasons, epochs, and eons. The wave-like movement of the Moon Goddess's realm spiraled and wound, twisting and repeating itself.

The imagery of the Goddess was blatantly sexual, relaying her damp, hidden mysteries. Dr. Vocatta George, in her dissertation *The History of the Goddess and the Transpersonal Significance of her Decline and Re-Emergence in the West,* explains that in the Goddess religions,

> Sexuality [including intercourse] was a sacrament, an integral part of many of the religious observances;...These rites practiced in the Holy Temple of the Goddess were a sacred acknowledgment, a submission to the laws of nature, sexuality and instinct. The seriousness of these holy acts and the laws governing them demonstrate the deepest values and meaning of the time.[6]

Seeing the miracle that women produced new life from within their own bodies, these people venerated them. They had an intense respect for nature and for women.

Goddess worshipers honored a feminine wisdom. Their deity encompassed paradox. She stood apart, impersonally bearing witness to the cosmic processes. Her laughter echoed through eternity somewhere beyond the reach of personal anguish. People yearned to see through her eyes, for in union with her they would be able to lose their painful awareness of themselves. They would lose their fear of death by knowing it as a transformative process. Once again identifying with the whole, they would welcome the inevitable cyclical changes of the seasons and of birth, life, and death.

Her wisdom was a knowing, not from the head alone but with the whole self—a knowing that could not be explained rationally.

> ...Not [as] an act of intellect, functioning as an organ for swift registration, development and organization; rather it has the meaning of a conception. Whatever is to be understood must first enter matriarchal consciousness in the full, sexual, symbolic meaning of a fructification.[7]

The whole being is involved. Neuman goes on, describing moon wisdom as "[encircling] what it conceives. It...admits everything into its totality and transforms it along with its own being. It is always concerned with wholeness."[8]

The reverence and worship of the Goddess filled a long period of history. Over a period of 2,000 years, beginning in the Bronze Age (about 1,500 B.C.E.) and lasting until the seventeenth century, Western civilization moved slowly toward Ego- or "I"-centered consciousness. They moved from matriarchal to patriarchal consciousness, from Yin to Yang, from Eros to Ego. People separated themselves from the erotic feminine. Making distinctions and noticing differences, their view of the world and their relationships changed.

Accompanying the shift toward the masculine, with its movement toward individualized consciousness, the conception of the deity gradually began to include male figures. Dr. Vocatta George points out that originally the Goddess was "parthenogenic," that is, conceived alone. She lived and ruled without help, often without any relationship to men at all. Then, in response to the emerging male energy, male companions appeared. Dr. George tells us that at this early time, the Goddess was typically accompanied by a male consort, often a son/lover. At first he was depicted as smaller than she, many times on her lap. In time he grew in stature to become a god in his own right. Eventually he overpowered the feminine and relegated the Goddess to a subservient role.[9]

As the energy of differentiation slowly gained strength, Western people continued to separate and genderize the qualities of the deity. Highlighting these differences they organized configurations of similar qualities which coalesced into separate goddesses and then gods. Through them, people paid homage to their own polytheistic nature.

Perhaps the most familiar examples of this polytheism were the Greek and Roman gods and goddesses. They carried out the larger-than-life energies which surge through humans. There was Aphrodite, direct descendent of the monotheistic Goddess. She emerged from the sea on a shell like love emerges from the unconscious: raw, hungry and sexual, as well as soft, sheltering, and compassionate. Then Athena appeared, springing like pure reason from her father's head, foretelling the future through her denial of any relationship with the nature Goddess. Jupiter, Neptune, and Pluto separated the totality of what had been Saturn's domain, further dividing and specializing. They each took their piece: Jupiter the heavens, Neptune the oceans, and Pluto the underworld.[10] Humans became absorbed in the passionate lives of these goddesses and gods, identifying with their loves and jealousies and with the battles they fought. Humankind wanted to know and explore all of its potential.

As Western people moved toward more separateness, they moved further from the feminine toward a masculine way of thinking. The powerful magnetism of history dictated change. By 1,500 B.C.E., polytheistic worship of the goddesses and gods began to give way to the worship of a male God.[11]

The transition from plural deities of both sexes to a singular masculine deity took many years. In "On the Moon and Matriarchal Consciousness," Erich Neuman says that the new patriarchal consciousness emerged and distinguished itself from matriarchal consciousness, taking an opposite and independent stance. One stance, Neuman explains, is identified with the heart, the other with the head and the Ego. One is the consciousness of the earth; the other transcends and abstracts. One separates and sets apart, while the other encircles and relates. Patriarchal consciousness defines itself by articulating and naming. It is Logos, not Eros.[12]

The emerging Judeo-Christian male God further ordered and separated. He was the ultimate namer. The Old Testament introduces him in this way: "In the beginning was the Word, and the Word was God."[13] The movement away from the synergistic "we" of the Goddess-worshiping civilizations to the separate "I" of the new God consciousness was accompanied by a new fear of one another. Instead of working for mutually shared goals, individual's goals took priority and people found themselves at odds with each other. This kind of oppositional and competitive thinking resulted in a need to control others and a power-over structuring of society. It became "me" versus "them" and clearly, according to this new logic, if I did not control them, they would control me.

Many of the cultural myths of the transition period between "We" and "I" consciousness describe how the Ego, or "I," saw the feminine as an enemy and struggled against her. Like the minstrels of medieval courts, these myths carry the haunting stories of separation, passing the allegory down through the ages. In these myths, the hero's mission is to awaken and slay the mythical dragon, that powerful, dark, and primitive creature who sleeps in the misty realms of the unconscious.

According to Erich Neuman, to the immature Ego, dragons are symbols of the devouring aspect of the mother, representing an unconscious pull to regression which would result in being swallowed up into symbiotic oblivion. Symbolically, humankind, at this time, believed it must do battle with the erotic within itself, separate from the great mother, and overpower her. In order to gain strength to slay the terrible mother, the hero identified with a heavenly father.[14]

Other myths prophesy the obstacles and unsolved problems of the hero's path. Among the most famous of these is the Grail Legend. In this tale King Arthur's knights leave the Round Table in quest of the vessel which contained the blood of Christ after his descent from the cross. This vessel represents the feminine chalice, which was lost in the religions dominated by the male God. Each knight sets off on his individual quest, splintering the symbolic collective represented by the circular shape of the Round Table in the myth. In the end, as was foretold by Merlin, the wizard, Percival finds the Holy Grail. But, significantly, he does

not return with it to his King and fellow knights.
Instead he renounces the world, becoming a hermit.
Thus Western people were left with a splitting of temporal from spiritual and the individual solution from
the collective.[15]

Although the teachings of Jesus reflected a deep
respect for feminine spirituality and for women, as
Christianity became politicized it lost most of its relationship with the feminine. As Christianity rigidified,
God and man became separate. Western people's relationship with their Deity changed from one in which
they celebrated their connection with the Goddess to
one in which they respected their distance from God.

Erich Neuman suggests one way of looking at history
is that God and people are involved in a cooperative
process of development or evolution. According to this
point of view, humanity moves jointly with its deity
toward the goal of full actualization. From this perspective the monotheistic, male God was an important step
in this process representing the necessary evolutionary
pull toward the development of "I" or Ego consciousness.[16] And it is true that both humanity and its God
were well on their way to becoming fully independent
individuals, distinct from their environment and from
one another.

In the beginning there were many diverse forms of
Christianity, each with its teacher preaching their
truth. These early sects had many similarities to the
nature religions which preceded them. Their beliefs
and practices were, in fact, closer to Goddess worship
than they were to modern Christianity as we know it.
Judging by the standards of modern Christianity, their
beliefs and practices were heretical.

The teachings of the Gnostics, who lived 100-150 years after the birth of Christ, serve as an excellent example. When scholars presented these written gospels, they gave the world the first complete and accurate information about the beliefs of the early Christians. What they said was so shocking and threatening to the modern Christian Church that it prohibited the gospels' release for many years. In her book, *The Gnostic Gospels,* noted religious scholar Dr. Elaine Pagels analyzes their teachings. She describes a faith which differs drastically from the Christian dogma accepted as truth today.

The Gnostics had a shockingly different understanding of the relationship between people and God. They also believed differently about the divinity of Jesus, his resurrection, and his relationship to women. They even told the story of the Garden of Eden from a different vantage point than traditional texts.

The God of the Gnostic Gospels was not a separate, transcendent male being—a wise old man with white hair and a beard. More like the Hindu Atman or Brahman, their God was the ultimate ground of all being, the source. This source, drastically different from God as "master, lord, king, creator and judge,"[17] as he came to be known in modern Christian teachings, could be experienced by everyone. Anyone could know God. They did not need the hierarchy of priests, bishops, and popes to make their essential connection. *Gnosos*, Dr. Pagels explains, is a Greek word meaning "knowledge." The Gnostic, then, is one who has come to "know" through a process of insight and intuition. "To know oneself at the deepest level," they wrote, "is to simultaneously know God."[18]

Contrary to the fundamental creed of the modern Christian church, the Gnostics did not recognize Christ's divinity in the unique way the New Testament declares. The Gnostics suggest Jesus was the son of God as we all are sons and daughters, divine in our essential nature, a spark of the whole. While this belief may seem innocuous in the light of our modern familiarity with Eastern philosophies, we need to remember that since that time, thousands of people lost their lives in religious wars and conflicts for holding this belief.

Dr. Pagels tells us that in addition to this apostate view of Christ, the Gnostics did not take the Resurrection literally either. Actually, they referred to a literal view as "the faith of fools."

> The resurrection, they insisted, was not a unique event in the past: instead, it symbolized how Christ's presence could be experienced in the present...those who announced that their dead master had come back physically to life mistook a spiritual truth for an actual event.[19]

They go on to explain that this external experience appears as a vision received in dreams or trances. When the Apocalypse of Peter was discovered at Nag Hamadi, it told how Peter, "deep in trance, saw Christ, who explained, 'I am the intellectual spirit, filled with radiant light.'"[20]

The Gnostics also held the unorthodox belief that it was Mary Magdalene, not Peter, who was the first to see or experience Jesus in this visionary way. Heretical as it may sound, the Gospels clearly state Mary Magdalene had visions and insights equal to Christ's. According to the Gospel of Mary,

> "Peter invites Mary to 'tell us the words of the savior which you remember.' But to Peter's surprise, Mary does not tell anecdotes from the past: instead, she explains that she has just seen the Lord in a vision received through the mind, and she goes on to tell what he revealed to her."[21]

Not only does the Gospel of Mary suggest a drastically different conception of mystic or divine revelation and question the singular authority of Jesus, it also questions the sexual purity of Jesus as it hints at a sexually intimate relationship between Jesus and Mary Magdalene.

These examples clearly indicate a different place for women in the religious hierarchy than that of the Christian Church of today. The Gnostic interpretation of the story of the Garden of Eden also attests to their reverence for women and a belief in a feminine deity. The feminine reigned alongside the masculine. The Gnostics speak of the God who related to Adam and Eve as only a lesser deity. He is not, they say, the primary God, but one who arrogantly wants to believe he is. This God does not want Adam to know of his deceit, but to believe that he is the ultimate God. So, this lesser male deity forbade Adam to eat of the tree of knowledge. He became arrogant, saying,

"I am God and no other exists but me." But
when he said these things, he sinned against
all the immortal ones...When Faith saw the
impiety of the Chief Ruler She was
angry...She said, "You err, Samuel [blind
god]; an enlightened humanity [Anthropos]
exists before you."[22]

In the Gnostic version of the Garden of Eden story,
the serpent and Eve were actually the emissaries of
Sophia. Sophia, reminiscent of the great Goddess, was
the name given to the feminine Goddess of wisdom. She
was the counterpart of the male deity, his companion,
wife, or mother. Sophia intentionally sent the snake to
awaken Adam and to infuse him with a desire to
"know," in the Gnostic sense, the ultimate source. So
rather than Eve and the serpent being the negative, evil
causes of Adam's downfall, the Gnostics render them
honorable as guides to wisdom. It was only the later
Christians who changed the story, turning Eve into the
dark character who tempted man to disobey God. The
modern interpretation of the story marks the shift of
the role of women in religion as well as in the structure
of society. The Western view of women changed from
seeing them as wise and respected, to seeing them as
weak and contemptible.

The progressive deviations from belief in feminine
wisdom were not isolated or independent events. They
have a pattern and reflect the historical transition
taking place in people's relationship to the Deity and to
one another.[23] The shift from feminine to masculine
took many years. Although there were still some out-
posts of Goddess worships as late as 400-500 C.E., by
200 C.E. the reign of the feminine was largely over. Dr.

Pagels emphasized that feminine wisdom, in fact any feminine symbolism for the Deity, is markedly absent in the major modern religions today.[24]

But before the masculine could ascend to the throne, the Queen had to be dethroned, and the task was enormous. She permeated every part of life; in fact, life and the Goddess were synonymous. The patterns of life were drawn in reciprocity with her. Worshiping her was, in essence, a way of being in the world. It was the substance of everyday existence.

Feminine consciousness had to be changed within each and every person for the transition to be complete. Feminine icons had to be smashed and religious rituals forbidden. But Goddess worship was not just statuary and rite. The shift to masculine consciousness changed the very thought process and conception of life.

People achieved these nascent shifts in consciousness in a concrete and direct way. The bearers of this new consciousness met the feminine with a thrusting, driving, masculine force, beginning with the nomadic tribes sweeping down over the peaceful agrarian communities and beating them into submission.

To maintain an objective perspective, we have to step back from the often unquestioning acceptance of the Old Testament and the actions taken by the believers in its God. Justifying the brutality as a holy war, the nomads executed a determined campaign against the Goddess worshipers in the name of Yahweh. The Old Testament books of Judges, Kings, Jeremiah, Ezekiel, and Samuel contain accounts of battles which lasted hundreds of years against the followers of the more ancient religions, prejudicially referred to as "pagan" in the texts.

> Hebrew tribes, sanctioning their brutality
> with the orders of Yahweh, destroyed the
> Goddess-worshipping country of Canaan...
> Yahweh speaks: "Ye shall destroy their alters,
> break their images and cut down their groves,
> for thou shalt worship no other God, for the
> lord whose name is jealous, is a jealous
> God."[25]

He would not tolerate any departure from his dictates. When the people wouldn't give up their faith they were killed. In Jeremiah 44 there is "an account of the Lord's vindictive anger toward the women who burned incense and poured out libations to the 'Queen of Heaven.'"[26]

The historical shift in consciousness was an imperative. Those who brandished the new monotheism condoned any means which would accomplish their goal. In her dissertation, Dr. George refers to a passage in II Kings which tells how in 800 B.C.E.,

> Jehu seized the throne of Israel after murder-
> ing their "pagan" queen following the betrayal
> of her eunuchs. He tricked the followers of
> Jezebel [the Priestess of the Goddess] by call-
> ing for an assembly of the worshipers in their
> holy temple. When the shrine was filled and
> they were administering the sacrament, Jehu
> ordered his men to massacre the whole con-
> gregation.[27]

Later, when the Christians took up the evolutionary banner, the masculinization of relationships continued. In opposition to the teachings of Jesus, these soldiers of cultural change marched through history perpetuating a Machiavellian strategy in which the ends justified the means. They continued the violence against the feminine. They introduced their own skillful variations on the theme of control and domination by using power and fear. Through shame and humiliation they rallied against the remaining nature worshipers. So spellbound were they by "I" consciousness that men felt justified in killing hundreds of thousands of "heathen infidels" in the name of the church.

When the rumbling and quaking began to settle down, the shattered structure of society fell into a new configuration. People took on a linear relationship to their world and those in it. The nature of their relationship to God, to their environment and to one another became a hierarchy of power-over. Those scurrying up the power ladder thought nothing of stepping on the fingers of the people just beneath them to maintain their own position. They held on to their positions with a growing paranoia.

When people related to the God, they were no longer free agents, capable of their own divine revelation. "Whoever 'sees the Lord' through inner vision can claim that his or her own authority equals or surpasses that of the Twelve—and of their successors."[28] No longer an individual experience as it had been for the Gnostics, connection to God became the privilege of an exclusive few. Popes, bishops, and priests became the rank-ordered intermediaries who held the power. They would speak to God and experience Him for their supplicants, when and if they chose to.

The new hierarchy of the Church could not tolerate the early Christians' beliefs. The Church fathers claimed to inherit their authority from Peter, through direct lineage. Peter, they professed, had first authority because Christ appeared to him first after his resurrection. "Gnosis," or personal revelation, a direct experience of Christ, threatened their power and the entire religious and political hierarchy they had set up. Giving one's own personal experience credence and precedence over formalized religious experience was intolerable to them. Such views became obvious heresy.

Religious, political, and domestic functions were defined and limited. Relationships took place within a dominant-subordinate structure. The priest could talk to God and would pass his word on to the people. Men and women were given separate roles, complete with designated ways to behave, think, and feel. The church fathers created laws to define and fix these new relationships to protect and defend their power positions.

Women became the symbolic carriers of all of the feared natural instincts. Christianity, with its male trinity, officially canonized the male spirit in its Father, Son, and Holy Ghost trinity. Only chaste, virginal, or maternal Mary remained as a feminine symbol for Christians. The profound and obvious—and intentional—absence of the ancient wisdom of Sophia or the Moon and Nature Goddess is important here. Qualities that were considered feminine in men and women alike became shameful.

Eve's role in the Garden of Eden myth changed from the emissary of Sophia bringing wisdom, to the emissary of the Devil, tempting the man to turn away from God. With blatant sexual overtones, women became distinctly and solely responsible for the "fall of man." Celibacy and chastity were highly valued by the newly established Christian hierarchy. They translated

"Sacred Harlot," the Priestess of the Temple in ancient times, into "whore," with the all the connotations of her shameful fall from grace. Mary Magdalene lost her place as a visionary equal to Christ and was relegated to the role of temptress.

It is important at this point to avoid the temptation of using masculine and feminine as only the "symbolic magnitudes" that Erich Neuman refers to in "On the Moon and Matriarchal Consciousness." For in actuality, as the male God ascended to his throne, the gender issue was not just symbolic, it was substantive. Real women, daughters and wives became the focus of all the fear and insecurity people felt about their frail and separate identities. Society lashed out against women with overt, cruel violence. In *Complaints and Disorders: The Sexual Politics of Sickness,* the authors use the attitude of two early church fathers to exemplify this violent hatred.

> "Every women ought to be filled with shame at the thought that she is a women," wrote Clement of Alexandria, [who lived 150-215 C.E.]. And St. John Chrysostom (347-407)... pushed a woman off a cliff to demonstrate his immunity to temptation, [concluding with seeming pride]..."Among all the savage beasts none is found so harmful as women."[29]

From Tertullian, (190 C.E.) whose writings helped divide true believers from heretics in the early years of Christianity, we understand clearly the weight of the feminine crime.

"And do you not know that you are each an Eve?...You are the Devil's gateway. You are the unsealer of the [Forbidden] Tree. You are the first deserter of the Divine Law....On account of you...even the son of God had to die."[30]

And we can trace the punishment back to Paul, who said, "the women should keep silence in the churches. For they are not permitted to speak, but they should be subordinate...it is shameful for a woman to speak in church."[31] "Women," agreed Clement, Bishop of Rome, "are to remain in the realm of subjugation" to their husbands.[32] Thus men became the jailers of the feminine soul.

Centuries after the death of Christ, the violence against the feminine raged on. The church fathers had all but forgotten his message of love and compassion. Beginning in the eleventh century and lasting into the seventeenth century, hundreds of thousands of women suspected of nature worship were burned at the stake as witches—in the name of Christ. One man, a Lutheran witch hunter, bragged of burning 2,000 women himself. In England over 30,000 women were killed during these witch hunts. And in France an entire town of women clasped hands and walked into the sea, preferring to drown themselves rather than inform on one another and then watch as their sisters and friends were persecuted and burned at the stake.

So the tradition of violence against the feminine began and was sustained from generation to generation. It has continued into modern times in even more subtle and insidious forms, where few of us, women included, recognize all the ramifications. Those who are brave enough to point out the misogynistic attitudes and discriminatory practices of our modern culture are often ostracized and ridiculed. Think about it: How many times have you anticipated an exasperated sigh or a disgusted look and decided not to bring attention to an inequity or patronizing remark about women?

Why did people have to be so violent? What rationale could possibly sanction such an ardent and continuous attack on the feminine? The answer to these questions lies in understanding how fearful people's fragile identities were of being overwhelmed by the Great Mother. The pull to Goddess consciousness was always present and interpreted as a constant threat. Our ancestors struck out against the seductive power of the Great Mother, believing they must steel themselves against her hypnotic call.

They believed the Great Mother had many disguises. They needed to be alert, watching for her everywhere. She might appear as a siren, beckoning to them, seducing them back into symbiotic oblivion. The regent Goddess might come to them disguised as primal desire and sensual pleasure, luring them to succumb to their instincts. The addictive dangers of her treasures were obvious. Risking an occasional indulgence in her erotic pleasures, they chanced falling into ecstasy, never to return. The result would be lives out of control, progress and productivity arrested.

Or the Goddess might come to the unsuspecting in the form of intuitions and vague, irrational thinking. Disguising herself in the robes of vision and dream, she would lead the innocent to the palaces of the unconscious where they might circumambulate for eternity. She might appear as receptivity, lulling them into a yielding attitude, eroding their determination. But whatever the manifestation, the source was always clear, and clearly dangerous. People learned through the ages to be vigilant and respectful of her ever-threatening power. As they checked their neighbors and themselves for any sign of her emergence, altered states became mental illness, nature worship became paganism and idolatry, while awe and reverence of the Goddess turned into anxiety and dread.

Explained according to the developmental paradigm of Sigmund Freud, during the period when feminine consciousness shifted to masculine, individual identities, or Egos, were very new and unstable. People were not sure they could trust the boundaries they had established to define themselves. Freud described the interpsychic situation this way. He called the individual identity the "I" or "Me," which was translated into English as Ego. The internalized voice of the male power structure, the demanding voice of authority from above, Freud called the "over or above I." We know it as the Super Ego. The voice of internal desire he called the "it," which we know as the Id. An oversized Super Ego clamped onto the unmanageable Id with an iron grip. It puffed itself up to the height it felt necessary to handle the unwieldy desires of its prisoner. The Ego had an overseer (the Super Ego) who, even though it lashed out repeatedly with its whip of "should"s and rules, could barely keep the Id's erotic desires under control. Under these threatening conditions, the Ego was never confident of the stability of its existence. Freud explained the violence against the feminine as the result of an insecure Ego attempting to satisfy the needs of the Id under the harsh judgment of the Super Ego.

Lawrence Kohlberg, in his extensive study in the area of human moral development, gave an explanation of the violent attack on the feminine from a slightly different perspective. He answered the question, "Why did people take on the rules and values of those in authority and defend these values with such fierceness?" He described this kind of adherence to rules as typical of certain early stages in human development. He explained that, in the preconventional and conventional stages, people will adhere to authority either out of fear or because they have identified with those in power.

> At the preconventional level a child adheres to the rules out of fear of the consequences of breaking them...At the second major level, the conventional,...the child is inclined to follow the dictates of established authority.[33]

When considered in the light of Kohlberg's sequence of moral development, this violence against the feminine was committed out of a combination of fear and compliance. Either people were terrorized into compliance with the perpetrator or, like many of the victims of concentration camps, people identified with their captors and actually took on the belief systems of the male power structure, thus perpetrating the power-over relationship.

Kohlberg went on to say that, in the final stage of moral development (reached by only a few), a person makes choices according to universal ethical principles which go beyond the dictates of society. Only at this stage can a person support taking action against the cultural norms or demonstrate a flexibility beyond a "law and order" orientation.

Does this mean that those of us who take issue with the power-over relationship norms of our society have reached a morally advanced stage? Are we finally allowing ourselves to reconsider the dictates of our captors? Are our Egos now confident enough to begin to loosen the iron grip of our Super Egos and liberate the feminine? But please wait. Before we become too enthralled with our moral superiority, there is something we should consider.

In her revolutionary book, *In A Different Voice*, Carol Gilligan questions the universality of the developmental model which Freud originated and Kohlberg perpetuated.[34] She brings our attention to the fact that a feminine view of morality is entirely different. Gilligan's research indicates that women value relationship. They value communication and responsiveness, which, when measured by Freud's or Kohlberg's standards, minimize women's moral development. Both Freud and Kohlberg value independence and autonomy. Freud's goal was the development of an independent identity; Kohlberg's goal was independent thinking, uninfluenced by the cultural imperative. Women's vulnerability and dependency, their use of compromise as the mode to solve moral dilemmas, seems immature when measured against Freud's standard of independence or Kohlberg's criterion of systematic thinking and the impersonal examination of logic for determining moral truths. According to Gilligan, women might not even consider our current challenge of male authority as a high moral achievement. Instead they might be prone to suggest a communication of difference, expecting a compromise for the common good.

We have used the wide-angle lens of history to follow the progressive changes in relationship. It is important to remember, though, that history itself is embellished with its teller's cause-and-effect perspective. If we step back for a moment, we will see that history is no more than a cultural myth, a collective dream. The way the myth is told, or the dream interpreted, gives meaning to the sequence of collective events. Although the interpretation of the story or dream seems to be logical, it is not a moral imperative. Historians, philosophers, and theorists are storytellers. We tend to accept the reasoning they use to connect the events in their story not only as truth but as the standard we use to measure our progress.

The developmental model can become just such a standard. The danger of laying the developmental model over history is in sanctioning the violent attack on the feminine as necessary for "progress." Then the assumption is that masculine, individualized "I" consciousness is a higher consciousness than the feminine and that the power-over model was what brought about that higher consciousness.

Fortunately, if we use a feminine viewpoint, we do not have to choose between Freud/Kohlberg and Gilligan, or between one view of history and another. We don't have to decide whether a morality based on logic and independence is superior to one based on the importance of relationship. Using a feminine perspective, these seemingly contradictory values can be seen as interconnected and complementary.

II.
SCIENCE

Like the day or the year in nature, so every life, indeed every cycle of experience, is a continuity by which old and new are linked together.[1]

Emerging from backstage, standing erect, dapper in his starched white shirt and black tails, the man of science stepped up to the podium. He bowed to a round of applause, took up the baton, and after tapping it several times, began to orchestrate the next three hundred years of history. The music he conducted was dramatic and involving, in fact mesmerizing. People became totally immersed in its powerful rhythms and progressions, taken up into its reality.

This man of reason did not have humble beginnings. He was taken with his power and optimistic about his future from the start. He entertained the idea that the mind had unlimited capabilities and that people could use their mind to control their environment.

Science relieved the Church of the conductor's baton with enthusiasm—one might even say with a vengeance. But while the former conductor had been replaced, the new leader of the orchestra picked up the old familiar themes of separation and control. He wanted to transcend his animal nature. He resonated with the Church's belief "that casts objectivity, reason and mind as male, and subjectivity, feeling and nature as female."[2] The scientist was an innovative and creative conductor, and he developed these themes with his own personal variations, giving them new and broader meaning and expression.

In *Reflections on Gender and Science,* Evelyn Fox Keller suggests that many historians recognize the Royal Society as the father of modern science. She quotes Francis Bacon, its founder, as saying that the Society marked the "masculine birth of time" that would issue in a "blessed race of Heroes and Supermen"—a force that could "hound, conquer and subdue nature," "shake her to her foundations," "storm and occupy her castles and strongholds."[3]

She goes on to say that the Society's purpose, as explained by its secretary, Henry Oldenberg, was "to raise a masculine philosophy...where the Minds of Men may be ennobled with the knowledge of Solid truths."[4] With the birth of science, people now understood control to be more than inhibiting their instinctual behaviors. They understood that they must not only live separated from nature but make her serve them. Their evolutionary hero was no longer fighting dragons, dressed in armor and wearing the colors of his courtly lady. He now donned the crisp white coat of research and went to the laboratory where he battled bacteria.

The Judeo-Christian tradition moved Western people away from the experience of and even the belief in a participatory truth.[5] Science, expanding this distance, made objectivity, separation from subjective experience, its foundation. The more detachment *one* gains, the less personally or emotionally involved *one* is, the closer *one* will come to discovering the true nature of the universe. Where earlier seekers of truth like the Gnostics emphasized illumination through direct experience, mechanical scientists like Bacon and his followers emphasized the dispassionate discovery of truth through a rational mind and the scientific method. Like a Christian priest, the mind must be pure, separated from desire, both physical and emotional, to avoid contamination.

As the Dark Ages came to an end, for the first time in history Western people celebrated the "power of man." They no longer felt restricted to the redemptive themes of the church. They felt hopeful. Renaissance artists infused their paintings with light, depicting this potent optimism. They sculpted people as bigger than life—strong, confident, and perfect. Science now found it necessary to separate itself from religion in order to keep its basis in reason and objectivity and its belief in the empowerment of humankind. To the man of reason, even Christianity, with its hierarchy and its growing distance from nature, was too personal and subjective. Furthermore, the Church discouraged questioning and encouraged subservience. Questioning was the essence of the scientific method and the new people were the center of the universe, subservient to no one.

Never before in the history of civilization had the search for an understanding of life been so distinct from nature and religion. The closest we can get to a scientific ancestor prior to this new hero might be the ancient alchemist. In *The Anatomy of the Psyche*, Dr. Edward Edinger proposes that the alchemist did not separate himself from mysticism in his scientific inquiries. The image of his hooded figure bent over his ovens and steaming cauldrons foreshadowed the emergent "man of reason" in his intent to discover the nature of matter. His pursuit, however, in direct contradiction to mechanical science, depended on mystical/religious experience for success. Their process, called the "opus," was sacred, mysterious, and highly subjective.[6] Alchemists were wizards and mystics engaged in a search for the supreme and ultimate essence of matter.

Dr. Edinger goes on to describe the alchemical process in depth. He explains that the goal of the process was to produce gold from ordinary metals and an enlightened being from an ordinary person. "The procedure is, first, to find the suitable material, the so-called *prima materia*, and then to subject it to a series of operations that will turn it into the Philosopher's stone."[7] This process was symbolic of the final goal of life, the transformative experience. In the steam of their cauldrons and the ashes of their fires, these wizards looked for the one and indivisible essence of matter: God made manifest. Religion, personal revelation, and science were all one to them. "...Upper and lower and inner and outer were linked by hidden connections and identities. What happens in heaven is duplicated by what happens on earth..."[8]

Evelyn Fox Keller shares Edinger's view that the alchemists were hermaphroditic in approach and symbolic in method. They venerated Eros, the connectedness valued by the nature and Goddess worshippers. In fact, the symbol for the *conunctio*, the final stage in the process, is the sexual joining of the King and Queen depicted in alchemical texts. Even as physicians, the alchemists were hermetic, believing that "'the art of medicine is rooted in the heart' — that one 'discovers the curative virtues of remedies by 'true love.'"[9]

By the beginning of the Renaissance, the alchemists, with the exception of the few who continued their mystical search underground, turned toward a more concrete chemistry. By the time Francis Bacon and his cohorts founded the Royal Society, there wasn't a hooded figure among them. There was no veneration of Eros. Instead, the focus was on power and domination. Nature would be broken and domesticated. Matter would be "both tamed and conquered."[10]

Never before had this search for understanding created such a rift in people's relationship with the Deity. In their primal consciousness, there had been no separation between Nature, the Deity, and themselves. They were one. From their first moment of self-awareness, that moment of separation from the all-encompassing "one," they saw Nature as separate and feminine and glorified her as the Goddess. They wanted to be synchronized with her power. At this beginning stage, the relationship with Nature, Goddess, and each other was as an "I" to a "Thou." "The relation to Thou was direct. No system of ideas, no foreknowledge, no fancy, intervened between the I and Thou."[11] Even though the relationship was direct, it marked a significant separation.

As people evolved in their search for understanding, they gradually became more figural against the background of being. More and more there was a separate "I" and a separate God. In their relationship with the monotheistic male deity, a whole system of laws and hierarchy of officials intervened between them and their deity. Their scientific hero took this still somewhat tenuous tear in the fabric of wholeness and rent the garment in two. On one side was nature, an object to be analyzed from a safe and rational distance. On the other was the scientist. Relationship was now firmly established as an "I" to an "It."[12]

The relentless magnetism of power was so strong that people willingly turned away from some of the most vital parts of their lives. No more guilt-free abandon to the ecstasy of their emotions, their bodies, or even their connection with the divine. They sensed how essential to their progress it was that they gain control of themselves. The task was to become dispassionate, neutral, and objective. Emotions and desires could defile the truth. It took discipline and concentrated effort. They must not get lost in the senses but continually focus on the mind. The montrum they repeated was the scientific method: Stand back, observe, question, hypothesize, then intervene. Accurately note observations so that you can compare the data from before and after the intervention in an unbiased way. The data from this procedure would confirm or reject the hypothesis. The goal was to control for personal bias. The conclusions would be true because they were devoid of human prejudice.

Authorities throughout society repeated and taught this montrum. The discipline was effective, and this logical, sequential thinking became largely habitual. Gradually it permeated the structure of societies' perspectives, values, and beliefs. Although people heard voices calling them back to nature, like the romantic poems of Keats and Shelly or the art of the naturalists, the scientific stance held firm. It largely defined the relationship of people to the deity, of men to women, parents to children, co-worker to co-worker—everything and everyone, eventually including, of course, the relationship of counselor to client.

Scientific values promoted autonomy, independence, power, and control. Culture was specific and intentional in labeling these qualities as masculine and their opposites as feminine. The founders of the Royal Society did not consult *The Handbook of Non-Sexist Writing* before making their pronouncements; the stage was set. The lines these historical actors spoke were not just "scientific rhetoric. They were deeply embedded in the structure of scientific ideology."[13] Woman, who once played the coveted role, the venerated symbol of uroboric wholeness, promptly found herself cast in the decidedly unfavorable role of sinful temptress.[14] At first the part only called for her to lure the leading man, who played the innocent victim, away from obedience to God's law. But against the backdrop of scientific rationality, the director developed her character further. He wanted the message to be less vague, to leave less to the imagination. It must be clear that it was

Eros—involvement, emotions, and runaway instincts—that was to blame for the fall of the leading man.

With the female lead locked into a diminished character, the director turned his attention to expanding and elaborating the leading man, developing his character into a being of mind and spirit, lofty in ideals, separate and uninfluenced by emotion. He was taught that "truth has no chance when 'the affections wear the breeches and the female rules...'"[15] People coached themselves to resist real communion with whatever they related to, be it their Deity, their science, or other creatures of the universe including each other.

They polarized the sexes, overlooking the androgynous character of humanity: the masculine present in every woman and the feminine present in every man. They placed man in an authoritarian position over women, as they had mind over feeling. They believed men to be superior to women, not only morally as the church did, but intellectually as well. Both men and women devalued and rejected their feminine qualities of emotionality, instinctual needs, and the need for intimacy and connectedness. In the process they not only objectified nature but relationship itself. Man was object to woman, woman was object to man, and relationship, like nature, became something to study and analyze from a distance.

Let's revisit our scientific hero, still in his white lab coat, meticulously noting his observations while he wages war with bacteria. The rules of warfare: absolute autonomy. He must be uninfluenced by any of his own past experience or preconceptions. Further, even though he is part of a scientific team, he must be equally uninfluenced by the input of his colleagues.

Autonomy is his value, and it is that kind of autonomy that "can be bought only at the price of unrelatedness."[16]

This scientist, like the dragon-slaying hero of old, wants to dominate and control. He is engaged in a battle with bacteria. He means to overpower them and cleanse humankind of the scourge. His attitude in the laboratory generalized throughout his life, and relationship became an arena for power and domination.

The dynamic of relationship mirrored the new scientific values. Governing each relationship was a central authority. It was the male God, the CEO, the father or husband, and he ruled with absolute power. Before blaming the woman for being a passive victim or the man for being abusive, keep in mind that at this time in history there was a tacit cultural agreement that this structure was for the best. It promoted safety and security. Its organization was static. People knew what to expect. No disorder or chaos should occur. In hopes of reaping the benefits from this order, both men and women agreed to honor and promote the masculine and devalue and suppress the feminine—both in society in general and within each individual as well.

Women held the same values as men for rationality over emotionality, for the mind over the body, and for the masculine over the feminine. This agreement affected the flow of history and changed consciousness. At first the inequality was maintained by a primitive violence. Eventually, as women sank deeper into a passive depression and dependency and men rose into an inflated arrogance, blatant force was no longer necessary. The same effect was rendered by the cultural pressure to accept and identify with with the roles. Finally people came to enjoy them and believe them to be authentic.

Language itself demonstrates how firmly embedded this tacit agreement was in the culture. As spoken consciousness, language reflects thought, perception, and understanding of reality. Probably only a few readers of this book, male and female, questioned the use of *his*-story throughout the preceding pages. In *The Handbook of Non-Sexist Writing*, the authors cite English as an example of language as a reflection of masculine consciousness.

> The reason the practice of assigning masculine gender to neutral terms is so enshrined in English is that every language reflects the prejudices of the society in which it evolved, and English evolved through most of its history in a male-centered, patriarchal society.[17]

Relationship changed as people became more and more successful at pushing the hated and feared parts of themselves into the unconscious. Finally they split them off entirely and believed these parts were no longer theirs. People were hopeful that the "mind of man" would solve the problems of humanity. They agreed that their feminine qualities, behaviors, and even thoughts would impede the scientific effort and interfere with humanity's progress. If you have ever believed this—and most of us have believed it at some point—you understand the sincerity of the effort to suppress the feminine and the sense of mastery people felt when they were successful.

As evidence of the virtue of the effort, science offered one miracle after another. Human suffering was relieved by the cure of small pox, the discovery of penicillin, and the polio vaccine. The very dimensions of the universe were altered with the invention of the steam engine, the automobile, airplanes, and aero-space-craft. The world became a global village. And in the sequence of miracles, interpersonal space shrank to almost nothing. With the invention of the wireless, the telephone, and satellite relay, global communication became commonplace. Seemingly, the Royal Society's purposes were achieved. Nature was tamed and conquered, and the "minds of men" were ennobled with solid truths.

Despite these accomplishments, you will not find many dinner parties today where philosophers of the politically correct avant-garde would be likely to raise their glass in praise of modern science. You would be much more likely to overhear a pair from this circle expounding passionately about the ravaged ecosystem the age of hard science is leaving in its wake. They would be sitting in Tribeca eating California Thai, exchanging worries about toxic waste and fluorocarbons, marking the arrival of another consciousness.

With the wide scope of our evolutionary perspective, we can make out attitudes and events that foretold the death of each of the conductors. First the Goddess yielded her baton to the gods and goddesses, then to the Judeo-Christian monotheistic male deity. Then science took on the role. But each of the directors of humanity's symphony revealed their progressively weakening condition through extreme one-sidedness and the resulting violence.

The ritual maiming and killing in the final years of Goddess worship were obvious symptoms of her decay. The crusades, witch hunts, and the Inquisition revealed an insidious illness deep within the body of the Christian Church. Each had once been the answer, numinous with evolutionary energy. Their energies were so strong and powerful that they each ruled on for hundreds of years, even though terminally ill and riddled with internal decay.

Science blurred people's vision by waving the baton of logic and objective authority. People overlooked the resulting symptoms for many years, and the life-threatening illness went undiagnosed. Never did they suspect that the pure and chaste scientist in his antiseptic lab coat might succumb to the all-so-human vices of power and greed. It did not occur to them that he would ever use those bacteria growing in his petri dish for germ warfare. They didn't foresee that he could become greedy and sell his inventions at the expense of the world's water supply or ozone layer—even at the expense of his grandchildren's well-being. Society has only very recently become aware that the "I"- or "Me"-oriented motivation that has guided Western progress since the seventeenth century is working to its detriment. The arrogance that came hand in hand with the Western world's accomplishments made people naive about how much they could control. They were not yet aware that this overcontrol would lead to destruction from within.

But wait! We must realize the full implication of what we are saying and from what perspective we are viewing these transformations. This kind of conversation, like the one in Tribeca, in which we are considering the downfall of classical science, can only occur when

change is already underway, when we are already onto
something new.

The age of hard science is ending. We are in transition. Ideas and beliefs people held to so rigidly for fear
of being devoured by the call of the sirens are becoming
more flexible and expanding. In retrospect, with some
hindsight already, we are finding that the scientific
"truths" people believed to be universal and fixed, are
not so at all. They appear to be temporary understand-
ings, relevant to only a brief period in history.

We gained the distance to see from this vantage point
through an evolutionary shift in consciousness. There
is an unusual mix of people in the lead and a new kind
of scientist is among them. These modern scientists
find themselves in the company of rock stars and
mystics who are vocalizing the same shift. The force of
evolution makes strange bedfellows. Surprisingly,
these scientists are reaching their "new age" revela-
tions using the scientific method—that very method
with which former scientists created germ warfare and
other inventions that have come dangerously close to
destroying our ecosystem.

The same objectivity that demanded such a separation from the other, resulting in that extreme "I" or "Me"
attitude which allowed the destruction of our environment, is also pulling us out of this near catastrophe.
The carefully dispassionate, unbiased impartiality of
science was a double-edged sword that ultimately cut
through itself. While one edge was able to coldly slice
through connectedness and intuitive discovery without
feeling, the other simultaneously performed the same
surgery on the preconceptions and prejudices of scientific thinking itself. The method, so to speak, became
its executioner and savior at the same time.

A few exceptionally brilliant scientists were able to follow the scientific imperative of being truly unbiased and autonomous. They actually suspended all preconceptions and remained open enough to interpret their experimental results in a way that contradicted all the basic premises of science up to that point. These scientists not only challenged major theories; even more profoundly, they challenged the assumed and often unexpressed beliefs underlying them. This is a very difficult and subtle thing to do, because most people don't even realize they have these beliefs, let alone be open enough to question them. It was like challenging the belief that the earth was round when everyone could see plain as day that it was perfectly flat.

And what were the underlying assumptions which these innovative scientists challenged? They were the "man of reason's" most sacred conviction: the foundation of scientific thought. *First they challenged the concept of separateness itself.* This was the oldest and most central idea, the one with which science initiated its emergence: "I think, therefore I am."

Then these innovative, modern scientists made another painful jab at the core of scientific thought. *They challenged cause-and-effect thinking.* Science had used the predictions made possible by cause-and-effect thinking's linear logic to make order out of a seemingly chaotic environment, to give them the semblance of control. Now they sliced through the safety net of power they had so painstakingly woven to keep from plummeting into the void.

What they said in their experiments exemplified a newly emerging consciousness. Much as the presence of the wind is revealed by the movement of tree branches, the shift in consciousness through the scientific discoveries of the period can be similarly detected. The experimental results and mathematical proofs presented by these scientists conflicted with the then-accepted theory. In fact, they were diametrically opposed to it. Scientists, like many other vanguards of change, ushered in the new consciousness by being able to tolerate the intensity of paradox without relieving their discomfort with it through either blindness or denial. This tolerance of paradox allowed them to see the old and the new without rejecting one or the other. The greater consciousness that emerged was achieved through holding both old theory and new until a larger understanding, which incorporated them both, could be reached.

Many students of evolution use physics as the best example of this transformational scientific thinking. It is a good example for this discussion because physics is the study of relationship from a scientific perspective. Through understanding the discoveries of modern scientists and the thinking process these discoveries stimulated, we can clearly see how their understanding of relationship changed. Their discovery process fostered a new consciousness.

Gary Zukov in his book *The Dancing Wu Li Masters*, describes the historical progress of physics. As he elaborates, he points out that it is not only the New Age physicists who have been the radical thinkers of their day. It seems physicists have a history of challenging, accepted thought. The first thing the original physicists did was to strike out "boldly against the grip of medieval Christian scholasticism...They attempted to place 'man' at the center of the stage,....to prove to him that he need not be a bystander in a world governed by unfathomable forces."[18] Next they said that people could understand the universe and control it. Zukov explains, telling us, "It was Galileo who first quantified the physical world. He measured the motion, frequency, velocity and duration of everything from falling stones to swinging pendulums — (like the chandelier in his cathedral)."[19] Thus, he placed humankind firmly in the central position. When Rene Descartes developed "the fundamental techniques of modern mathematics giving us the picture of the universe as a Great Machine...,"[20] the world became understandable. People even felt a bit safer. "It was Isaac Newton who formulated the laws by which the great machine runs."[21] With a group of concepts such as these, it appeared people could have some control over the forces around them.

These men proposed ideas that were revolutionary and counterculture. They struggled with their colleagues and the "moral majority" of their time. The new ideas they put forth were not recognized by their society for their scope nor welcomed as harbingers of a new consciousness. In fact, out of their fear of change, those in power actually persecuted these early scientists. We need only call up the image of Galileo being thrown into a dark prison cell by the inquisitors to understand the risk involved in reporting these discoveries.

They each must have undergone a personal, internal struggle as well. Imagine the intense moral conflict Newton must have experienced when he realized that beliefs could be verified experimentally. This discovery undoubtedly caused him to wonder whether the things that he accepted on faith were true. Those things, like the ontological argument for the existence of God, were based on philosophical proofs carried out in the mind. People knew God existed because they were capable of fathoming the infinite. Now there were proofs one could see and measure. They could be verified with tangible evidence. They could be repeated with the same results each time. He could describe physical relationships based "upon sound experimental evidence, and nothing else."[22] Not logic, not faith, but substantiated, confirmed evidence.

Until that time, religion was based on faith, on a belief in a God who could neither be seen nor verified. He was not just a higher power. The existence of a higher power is easier to prove than a male, omnipotent God judging and monitoring individual lives. Newton must have struggled to reconcile his faith with his new belief that the criteria for validity is objective proof. "If it could not be verified experimentally, it was suspect."[23] This had to have challenged his belief in a God he could not see and a Church that had rules and laws which could not even be questioned. As it has with his modern counterparts, his deep inquiry into the nature of matter uprooted all that was holy before it.

By the seventeenth century and the founding of the Royal Society, scientists proclaimed that the universe runs in specific, comprehensible ways. They agreed that people were capable of understanding the laws governing the Big Machine, could thus predict and through prediction feel some semblance of control. It was then just human nature to try and figure out how creatively they could use this control. Who among them could pass up the temptation to see if they could get the Machine to work for them? However, we can't reduce the motives behind scientific progress to greed and lust for power, as many are tempted to do today. It was also human curiosity; scientists wanted to test the limits of their capabilities.

What people did with the uncomfortable contradiction between their faith and their science was split one from the other. The entire society behaved like a duplicitous two-headed monster, with each head turned away from the other, looking in its own, separate direction. The split enabled them to hold independent beliefs and to act in contradictory ways. They could be inspired while singing hymns at church, and at work scoff at those weak and fuzzy-minded believers in a faith which could not be verified. These two heads were connected to one body, commanding inconsistent behavior. On one hand people could act in concert with Christ's compassion and care for those less fortunate than themselves. On the other hand, they could produce progressively more advanced weaponry with which to stamp the meek out of existence and grab the spoils of victory for themselves.

Science told the world they would find an explanation for every natural phenomena. As it explained more and more, it supported the belief and hope that nothing was impossible. The church could not interfere with this optimistic illusion. The one head simply could not bring itself to turn to the other and say, "Something is very wrong here." So, science went off in its direction, doing the talking and believing all could be explained, and the Church had very little influence on the path progress took.

Even up to the present century, this scientific optimism prevailed. Zukov tells us that Albert Einstein, whom we think of as the ultimate example of expanded scientific thought, clung tightly to the belief that the rational mind could grasp a complete understanding of reality.[24] In spite of the fact that his experiments and mathematical theories contradicted this belief, he was sure that with enough effort and sound experimentation, science would be able to explain every natural occurrence. He himself was caught in the hypnotic trance of power and hope, the limited understanding of his time. Regardless of his own discoveries, he couldn't break through to see the far-reaching implications of his own work.

But some modern physicists were able to do just that; what it took was the ability to use both of these long-divided heads simultaneously. Zukov describes their process as they studied the behavior of subatomic particles. Their field is called quantum mechanics. They studied the theoretical existence of particles that no one could see, particles that are smaller than atoms which themselves cannot be seen even with the most advanced microscopes. The more they studied these particles, the more they understood that they didn't follow the same laws that explained the movement of the Big Machine, or the theories of Galileo, Descartes, and Newton. Zukov explains that following the course of the discoveries of quantum mechanics can help us understand how physics radically changed scientific thought, giving it a totally new understanding of the nature of relationships. In tracking their process, he shows how a new consciousness emerged, one which incorporates the known and the unknown, the provable and the unprovable, faith and science.

In the early 1900s, Albert Einstein proved that light was made of tiny separate particles called photons. This was in direct contradiction to a discovery made one hundred years earlier by another scientist who proved that light was made of waves—not waves made of tiny particles but continuous, unbroken waves.[25] Although over the years well-respected scientists had repeatedly duplicated the experiments of both these men, to their great discomfort no one could disprove either theory. Physicists who believed that everything could be explained were left with the kind of frustration that makes you want to smash the Rubik's cube when that one incorrigible side refuses to come up all one color.

What these new physicists did then was something very different. They turned in their crisp white lab coats for the black robes of a Zen Monk. They sat with the paradox in *zazen* (meditation), like a monk with a koan. They handled the problem in the way a roshi would advise a novice monk to handle something he couldn't understand: "Bite it at once! Chew it to the pith."[26]

Believing light is both a particle and not a particle or that light is both a wave and not a wave is a very Zen-like, non-scientific attitude. Old-school scientists must have joked among themselves, asking each other, "How many Zen monks does it take to screw in a light bulb? One to screw it in and the other not to screw it in. How many quantum mechanicists does it take to describe light? Two: one to say it's a particle and one to say it's not a particle. Ha Ha!"

But new physicists did not split off one contradictory result from another as their predecessors had. They also resisted the temptation to embrace one explanation and reject the other. In fact, they did not defend against the conflict at all. Instead they sat with the contradiction and endured the discomfort. "Light behaves like a particle and light behaves like a wave," these Zen-like scientists repeated to themselves throughout their day. Probably behind every daily habit they performed was the recurrent thought, "This can't be. It doesn't make sense. It isn't rational.

Particles and waves have different qualities. They behave differently." Finally, at the verge of going mad, they made the "quantum" leap toward a higher understanding. It was so elegantly simple. *Light is a particle and a wave*. It is both.

This resolution seems obvious to us now, as things always do in retrospect. But it was an impossible explanation for a man of science, who expected definitive laws and categories. With the acceptance of this contradictory truth, scientific thought evolved past the point described by the Zen roshi. "The reason those who search for the Way are unaware of its reality is simply because from the first they accept all their discriminations for true."[27] Scientists, having made this leap, bravely considered that the paradox true for light (wave and particle) might not be unique to light but characteristic of other discriminations they were so sure of as well. The winds of consciousness were changing, such that things could no longer be seen in an either/or way.

Zukov continues with his story describing these incorrigible scientists. With the same inquisitiveness that always seems to be getting humans into trouble, they couldn't just let it lie. Oh no, they had to ask one more logical question. "What makes light a wave in one experiment and a particle in another?" Their answer is another testimony to their courageous thinking. They said that what makes light a wave in one experiment and a particle in another is the experiment itself. In other words, *what scientists find depends on the experiment they do to discover it.*

To their credit, they said this with full cognizance of its shattering implications on the reliability of science. It made the touted objectivity of science a groundless boast. In essence, this discovery meant that experimentally proven laws and theories are not based on some ultimate truth. Rather, they are the result of personal bias. It is, after all, the scientist who chooses which experiment to do. The determination then, of whether light is a wave or a particle, depends upon the scientist's choice. Scientists, whether or not they are aware of it, get the results they set out to find. If they choose to repeat the particle experiment, light does all the things particles are supposed to do, proving light is a particle. But if they choose to repeat the wave experiment, light does all the things waves are supposed to do and none of the things particles do, proving light is a wave. With this new understanding, science could no longer claim the presence of an objective observer getting results uncontaminated by personal involvement. Recalling the Eros of their alchemical ancestors, the experimenter and the experiment had once again become one.

Zukov explains this beautifully, telling us that in quantum physics experiments, there is an observed system, like a photon—a tiny energy packet of light—in the region of preparation and an observing system in the region of measurement. The observing system is the environment surrounding the observed system, including the experiment chosen, and all its specifications, measuring devices, and measurements. The only point at which one observed system is actually seen is when it interacts with the observing system. So there is light traveling undisturbed from the region of preparation to the region of measurement. Before the scientist measures it, it has the possibility of being a wave and the possibility of being a particle. It also has an infinite number of other possibilities for which physics has not yet invented experiments to measure. Scientists, by taking the measurement the way they do, cause one of these infinite possibilities to become reality. Before they relate to it, it is just possibility. Quantum physicists had now plainly answered their question, "What makes light a wave in one experiment and a particle in another?" They did! They stated that "scientists create their reality by their relationship with it." They could no longer get an accurate picture of reality by distancing themselves from it. In fact, the opposite was true. Experimenters, in the ways they chose to measure, caused what they measured to exist.

So it seems that on the subatomic level, matter comes into existence in the form it does as a result of the nature of people's relationship with it. They only know what they know about the properties of matter through inference, through how it interacts with the observing system: themselves. "Properties belong to interactions, not to independently existing things, like 'light.'" *There is no separate reality,* no photon separate from the human observer. Things exist only in relationship to one another.[28]

The roshi told his students, "The entire world is the eyeball of a Buddhist monk...Take one more step!"[29] Zukov describes how quantum physicists took this next step toward an enlightened understanding of the connected nature of reality. In the now-famous double-slit experiment, they sent light through a screen that had one exposed slit and observed the lighted portion on the photographic plate behind it. Then they exposed a second slit and sent light through the screen and again observed the pattern on the plate. In the second instance they noted that the portion that had been lighted in the first instance was totally dark. This doesn't sound too revolutionary until we realize it means that when there were two slits, none of the light, neither a wave nor a particle, went through the original slit in the way it did when there was the only one slit. It is easy to rationalize this occurrence by saying that once light went through the two slits, it would diffract, creating a different pattern on the plate than it did when it only went through a single slit. With the double slit, one might try to make a case for the possibility that the diffracting light might completely miss the area that was lighted when there was only one slit opened. The scientists "chewed it to the pith" but found an enigma. In the second experiment, how did the very first light particle or wave know not to head directly to the photographic plate? How did it know to diffract when there was nothing there to diffract it yet? Did it somehow "know" there was second slit? How could it get this information?

In order to solve the enigma, the scientists used their Buddha mind. Once again they did not avoid the anxiety of accepting the seeming impossibility that the first light particle or wave had to "know" that there were two slits before it got there. So these scientists put themselves in the place of the first photon. At the moment they made themselves "one" with the photon, they reached an enlightened understanding: *connection!* They knew that because of the connectedness of all things, the photon had received the message instantaneously. There was no separation between the photons, the experimenters, or the photographic plate. They were all one and as such had access to the same information. The experimenters reached the same conclusion as a Buddhist monk would. Reality cannot be reduced to separate objects, each with an existence of its own. It is all one connected universe that "knows."

As the tallest trees in the forest are moved first by the wind, so the new consciousness was first received by scientists whose minds were open to it. And just like the branches of one tree moving those of another close to it, other scientists began to expand their inquiries into things that had never before been questioned. In *Reflections on Gender and Science*, Evelyn Fox Keller cites the biologist Barbara Mclintoc and the process of her discovery of genetic transposition as another example of how scientific attitudes changed. Her way of relating to the plants she studied was similar to that of the quantum physicists just described. She, as an innovator in the field of biology, was able to ease the rigidified boundary between subject and object. Like the physicists who bravely rode the light wave or particle rolling toward the double slits, Mclintoc describes herself as entering into the experience of the corn plants she studied. She avoided the pitfall of assuming that plants have nothing to say—an attitude that precludes relationship of any kind. Such a stance allows no reciprocity. People don't get any new information if they are not open to hearing it, which results in eliminating the possibility of learning that which differs from their preconceptions. So, Dr. Mclintoc found a monk's robe that fit her, put it on, pulled the hood over her head, and sat down to become one with these plants.

What she discovered when she did this contradicted the deterministic laws believed to describe genetic relationships. Biologists came from that same Newtonian genre physicists had, "a universe unfolding in strict causal sequence..."[30] They accepted and presumed, as all people did, that relationships were authoritarian and hierarchical. Biologists were monotheistic in their understanding of how genetic information was communicated in the living organism. For them, God was embodied in DNA. DNA issued the orders for form and function to the RNA, which passed them down through the ranks to the lowliest cell.

When Mclintoc sat, as in zazen, with the corn plants and patiently watched them with real curiosity, she found it didn't always work this way. She saw an organization of relationship that was considerably more rich and complex. She discovered that, in times of stress, "genetic elements can move, in an apparently coordinated way from one chromosome site to another..."[31] DNA actually responds to messages from the organism. It is not in sole command.

Dr. Mclintoc was able to see that the DNA had a different relationship with the corn plant because she had a different relationship with the corn plant. Both relationships permitted the rigid boundaries, the strict role definitions, and behavioral expectations between subject and object to fade. Her discoveries mirrored the relationship the physicists had with light. When separate, one finds separateness; when connected, one finds connection, or Eros. As the scientist allowed herself to merge with her subject, she came to know the experience of the DNA. She understood not as a separate, isolated entity but as a part of all that is connected with the corn plant. The relationship of the DNA to the corn plant, of the scientist to her experiment, changed from authoritarian to reciprocal. When boundaries diffused, information flowed. There was a different knowing that flowed from a place of interconnectedness.

Just like the quantum physicists who dared the mystical ride on light, Mclintoc discovered relationship to be global interdependence.[32] What people find in nature is subject to their relationship with it. Once, individuals had interacted as an "I" to an "It"; now they were able to relate as an "I" to a "Thou." "The thou meets me....I step into direct relation with it...All real living is meeting."[33]

The way these Zen-like scientists became one with their objects, making them subjects, is reminiscent of the alchemists and before them the Gnostics and Goddess worshippers who had experienced a participatory truth. These modern scientists also made their discoveries through Eros and its inherent dissolution of boundaries. But it was a very different experience from people's original state of undifferentiated unity. Scientists were coming back to Eros from a place of separation instead of starting there. In fact, they had finally become so secure in their individual consciousness that they could break the taboo and allow boundaries to dissolve once again. They embraced the devouring potential of Eros, safe in their ability to reemerge as separate individuals.

People have blended the best of the masculine—its ability to transcend preconceptions, its objectivity—with the best of the erotic feminine—relatedness. They have discovered a way to deal with that part of the masculine that twists and deforms and that terrifying part of the feminine that has to do with loss of self. They discovered that "order in nature is larger than the laws we can invent..."[34]

> The focus on order rather than law enlarges
> our vision of both nature and science. It
> suggests a way of thinking of nature as nei-
> ther bound by law nor chaotic and unruly,
> and of science premised on respect rather
> than domination, neither impotent nor coer-
> cive but as knowledge always is, inevitably
> empowering.[35]

Now humankind is free, part of the fluid dance of the Tao. The scientific hero has picked up a torch and joined the vanguard lighting the way into the twenty-first century. What scientists discovered about the interactive, reciprocal quality of relationship in physics and biology is true for the therapeutic relationship as well. It is time therapists stop their preoccupation with making their calling a science and notice where science is going.

III.
THERAPY

Hereby the nature of change is defined as change of the smallest part.[1]

At first I see a series of vivid images: a mother comforting a sobbing child; women laughing and taking around a kitchen table; a midwife delivering a baby; a half-naked priestess beating a drum. Then I am sitting with a client, my head bowed slightly. I wait, reverently, respecting his reluctance, confident the restorative disclosure will come. When the scene changes again, I become aware of the faint aroma of disinfectant hovering in the air. I can hear the muffled step of crepe-soled shoes passing behind my closed door. Soon the receptionist will usher my client into the room. From the seat behind my large mahogany desk, I feel confident. There is a soft rap on the door, and shaking myself awake I say, "I will be right with you." Surprised by my lucidity and quick recovery, I realize I have fallen asleep on my office couch and my next client has delicately announced her presence, interrupting my dream.

The images in this dream symbolize the richness and scope of the therapeutic encounter. Although the images are personal, they are true on the collective level as well. We can amplify their collective meaning by stepping back into our historical perspective for a few more moments.

The way our society defines the relationship between therapist and client has its roots firmly embedded in antiquity. If you were to see a Miller Analogy question stating, "Client is to therapist as blank is to blank," history would provide us with many fillers. It could well be, client is to therapist as patient is to physician; as parishioner is to priest; or as supplicant is to God. Society defines its roles, expectations, and goals from this set of historical givens. We did not select these roles from a wide range of choices. Rather, we inherited them.

The dream image of me sitting reverently with my client recalls the posture of the priest. Like the priest, I as a therapist hear confessions. The power to heal is in the knowing. Everything must be told. Like the confessor, I am not in the personal. I am the emissary of God, acting through the authority of the Church. Separated by the wall of the confessional, I quantify sins: venial or mortal. I dole out penance. People leave the confessional relieved. Someone in authority has told them what to do. They are able to go on with their lives. As for me, as for the priest, either I am actually a channel, a connection to the spirit, or a charlatan pretending to be one. But whether the connection is valid or not, I, like the priest, must act as if it is to fulfill my role in the relationship.

And what is the nature of this priest/supplicant relationship? It is one of the powerful to the powerless. Michael Fouchult, in *The History of Sexuality*, says confession is a "ritual that unfolds within a power relationship to a judging authority—or consoler."[2] "The agency of domination does not reside in the one who speaks...but in the one who listens..."[3] The confessees feel weak and unable to live as they should. But they hope the authority will be a forgiving one. Yet even forgiveness is compassion from a position of power. It is not as equals that people confess to the priest. For with equals, who is it that dictates what needs to be forgiven?

Not so different from the posture of the priest in the dream is the posture of the doctor. Both priest and doctor offer the security of authority to people—being told by someone who "knows." For me as the dream doctor, knowledge also equals power. My scientific medical training continues the obsession with knowing, adding to the priest's quantifying, "the formidable pleasure of analysis."[4] Where the priest's focus is on power over eternal life, the doctor's focus is on mastery of the present life. In warding off the threat of disease and death, the doctor comes a little closer to actually being God than the priest does. Also, like the priest, the doctor is the authority, listening and making judgments. Ferreting out the problem, he gives it a name and, like a penance, the patient passively follows the prescription. The hoped-for result: relief.

Within Western religion and science, personal gnosis was forgotten. Diagnosis took over. Knowing, which had once been an experience of melding, was now an experience of discriminating differences. Authorities examined problems, made their differential diagnosis, and gave their advice. Over time, the problems changed and the advice changed, but the authoritarian relationship remained the same.

It is important to mention that, even within this power dynamic, people were healed. These priests and doctors carried the healer archetype. A good part of their motivation was the sincere desire to respond to the human condition, to ease pain and suffering. And they were often successful.

The first people to think of themselves as therapists were physicians. These physicians brought the scientific model from their medical training into the consulting room. At the beginning of the nineteenth century (the same era of major changes in physics), we can recognize another vanguard scientist in Sigmund Freud. When we add his love of analysis and to his love of confession, he represents a hybrid of priest and scientist. He was the product of history but he was also the harbinger of change.

He identified himself with the accepted attitude of the day: authoritarian, detached, and objective. But he also responded to a collective spiritual need to connect the healer with the healed. Although he did not realize the full implication for the therapeutic relationship, by opening the tightly closed door to the unconscious, he began the process of connecting masculine reason with feminine instinct and interaction.

Like some of the other early twentieth-century scientists, Freud set out to explain that which could not be seen. He theorized that much of what we do, think, and feel is influenced by a powerful force of which we are not conscious. To him, the unconscious was that part of our personal history that lay outside our awareness. Even with this limited view of the unconscious, he was unwittingly and unconsciously turning down the path that would merge therapy with spirituality.

Just as Galileo and Descartes theorized that the universe was governed by laws we could understand, so Freud thought that the laws governing the human psyche could be discovered and understood. Further, he believed he could prove these laws scientifically through the clinical observations he made on himself and his patients.

Interestingly, his theory, later called Ego psychology, explained the nature of individual development in much the same way I describe collective evolution in this book: a sequence of efforts to separate from the feminine. His paradigm was scientific. It conformed with historical scientific thought and its definition of relationship. His approach was largely analytic and diagnostic, offering an assessment of health by an outside authority. Freud related to his "patients" from a therapeutic posture synchronized with the distanced scientific model of medicine. He valued the independent Ego, much as science honored the objective observer.

The primary value and the measure of health for the Ego psychologist is separateness. Human development is measured by "a critical sequence of separation from others."[5] Freudians measure maturity by the successful development of an individual identity. This independently functioning "I" that we think of as ourselves, he called the Ego. In utero and in the first few month of life, the tiny infant does not know itself as a separate being. Only slowly does it begin to identify itself as having an individual existence.

In the war for the development of an independently functioning "I," Freudians describe the separation from the mother as the crucial battle. The young Ego becomes more clearly defined through recognizing the difference between itself and mother. The more distinct, the better. The Ego's identity is strengthened by resisting the erotic relationship the mother represents. The maturing Ego must not give in to its need for relationship. Its development depends on resisting and defining itself as separate.

A constant state of vigilance and anxiety result from denying the need for relationship and defining health and maturity by degrees of separateness.[6] People have to resist their natural predisposition or attraction to relating through similarity. As in guerrilla warfare, people can never clearly identify the enemy. There is no final battle they can wage and be done with the war. Even when they overcome their enemy-mother, they are not safe. They cannot lay down their weapons because they must be alert to the next insurgence of their natural urge to connect.

Freudians say that although these impulses for connection do come from within, the developing Ego should not identify with them. People must control these impulses and keep them from interfering with their lives. The result of dealing with the anxiety produced by disowning and repressing these natural impulses is a rigid and dangerously fragile autonomy.[7] It is a maturity which is achieved through hyper-independence and a necessary preoccupation with control. It punishes weakness and rewards domination. By this definition of maturity, "people of both sexes can, and do, come to look to control of self and others as a means of bolstering their Ego boundaries and, simultaneously, their self-esteem."[8]

Certainly, when we were young (and really, if we are honest, just as much as time goes on), we realized that we would never be strong enough to withstand our attraction to relationship and synthesis. We needed help in our effort, and it could not come from mother. "'Against the threatening possibility of remaining in or sinking back into the structureless unity from which the Ego emerged, stands the powerful paternal force....'"[9] Just as people turn to the heavenly male God as their savior, so we turned to the earthly father for the help we needed. We projected onto him the power and control we knew our fragile Egos didn't possess. He, we believed, had mastered the separation and dominated the alluring feminine force. His domination was all-encompassing: economic, political, emotional, and spiritual. We identified and aligned ourselves with him. We could not question his authority because we believed it was our only hope.

His was the unquestionable voice of authority. He did not settle for close. He spurred us on toward perfection.

We called him lord and father. Freudians called him the Super Ego. He loomed over us like St. Peter judging at the gates of heaven, reminding us what was right action and right thought. Ever alert to our impulses, his was the inner voice with which we judged ourselves. His advice was filled with self-evident "shoulds." He was our personal connection with the Word of the Judeo-Christian Lord.

Freud thus depicted our evolutionary situation and its tensions on an individualized level. As above so below; as in the macrocosm so in the microcosm. The Ego has a difficult task, that of the mediator. It must attend to the pronouncements of the Super Ego, catch the erotic impulses of the Id, and try to maintain its integrity. Mother was the object from whom we must separate. Father was the person with whom we identified. We dealt with both the mother and father like hypothetical, archetypal powers,[10] never allowing ourselves to relate to them in the personal. We were constantly keeping people and the need for relationship with them at bay. We never gave ourselves the opportunity to discover whether we still needed to be so afraid of connection.

Freud, as he listened to his patients' confessions, discovered that the struggle between the Id and the Super Ego, between instinct and inhibition often played itself out in human sexual relationships. Freud defined as pathological that which the Victorians most feared—the feminine, the emotionality and sexuality of women. Not surprisingly, then, an analysis of the feared object—woman and her sexual life—became the basis for the development of Freudian theory. Women became the patients and their hysteria was the illness.[11]

Women were the patients, the "objects of study." In repressing them and their sexual and emotional responsiveness, Victorian culture gained safety and distance from the feminine in themselves, their erotic impulses and emotions. When the already over-compliant hysteric took her doctor's advice and tried ever harder to control her unruly emotionality, it pushed her even further into her "hysteria." The effects of this advice to repress and deny emotionality is exemplified in *The Yellow Wallpaper.* When the heroine implies that she is mentally unhappy to her physician husband, he, clearly out of fear, encourages her to control herself.

> "Really you are better!"

> "Better in body perhaps—" I began, and stopped short, for he sat up straight and looked at me with such a stern, reproachful look that I could not say another word. "My darling," said he, "I beg of you, for my sake and for our child's sake as well as for your own, that you will never for one instant let that idea enter your mind! There is nothing so dangerous, so fascinating, to a temperament like yours. It is a false and foolish fancy. Can you not trust me as a physician when I tell you so?"[12]

She listened, further repressed her passion, and stepped over the edge into madness.

Freud denied the reality of his famous patient Dora, much as this physician denied his wife's reality. He ignored the incestuous implications of her dreams, ignoring as well his earlier statement that "a later scene only owes its power to its relationship to an earlier one."[13]

According to Martha Knowell Evans in *Hysteria and the Seduction of Theory*, the analytic stance "plays a protective role for the analyst, safeguarding him against the traumatic effects of a devastating encounter with a female subject of desire...."[14] She makes the point that analytic theory itself acts as a defense, defending the therapist from an erotic encounter with the patient. The distance demarcated through objectification permits the analyst a certain comfortable protection from his own sexual and, in the broadest sense, erotic desire.

But in actuality, the woman and her Freudian analyst were very much focused on a sexual relationship. The psychiatrist as physician/priest encouraged the woman to confess the sexual traumas in her life, even her sexual feelings for the psychiatrist himself. He then analyzed these confessions, fitting them neatly into theory as fantasy or transference issues. As clever as his intricate system of denial was, the Freudian analyst was certainly deeply involved in a type of sexual relationship with his patient.

As Martha Knowell Evans suggests, theory functions as a distancing mechanism. It shapes the boundaries of the patient-doctor relationship. It prescribes the proper encounter. In this relationship the patient and doctor are safely distanced from their impulses. This distance offers security for them both. One must have respect for defense mechanisms. They develop for a reason. They protect something vulnerable, some part of us that needs defending. Through the distance provided by objectifying women, psychiatrists protected themselves from their own emotional responsiveness and from acting out sexually with their patients. The stronger and more rigid the defense, the stronger and more available the impulse underlying it.

Their theories also protected Victorian society from owning the violence it committed against women. In fact, the knowledge of this violence was so frightening and close to surfacing, it eventually caused Dr. Freud to altogether deny his patients' reality and the validity of their traumatic experiences. At first, Freud acknowledged in his "Aetiology of Hysteria" that in many of his cases the cause of the illness was actual sexual abuse. Even then, though, he could not bring himself to abandon the authority of the father figure and consider incest. Later, and after much pressure from his colleagues, he retracted even the suggestion of an actual rape as an hypothesis. Using theory to distance, Freud renounced his earlier beliefs and reduced the woman's experience to an anxiety-ridden, wish-fulfilling incest fantasy. [15]

Although Freudians prided themselves on their scientific objectivity, their attitude was not without its bias. The feminist scholar Keller points out that science is anything but neutral. It is biased toward theory and objectivity and away from the emotional and personal. With a staunch righteousness, the psychiatrist resisted relating to his patient on a personal level or in any way joining her in her emotional responsiveness.

But, at the same time these things were happening, the pure scientist in the psychiatrist—that part which could be objective and see beyond personal needs— began to understand that repression and denial themselves could cause pathology. They created a myriad of difficulties.

Cautiously and maybe unintentionally, because of or despite their distant and rational stance, Freudians responded to a collective spiritual need to connect the healer with the healed. By opening the door to the unconscious, they began the process of resurrecting the feminine and began to be aware of the terrible psychological problems the violence against the feminine had caused. Those people who took Freud forward into the twentieth century both popularized and stereotyped his work. As they did, analysis, like religion, lost some of its numinous power and took on an exaggerated form.

Bruno Bettelheim, a contemporary of Freud's, explains that the translation into English of Freud's theories rendered what was humanistic and compassionate in Freud into what was cold and devoid of feelings. The German word "ego" means "I" or "me," the word "id" means "it," and "super ego" means "over I" or "above I." Bettelheim points out that the use of scientific terminology transformed Freud's introspective and reflective tendencies into a behavioral science.[16] While Freud's office was filled with symbols that were meaningful to him, the modern analyst's office is kept empty except for the couch and chair.

Robert Langs is a modern psychiatrist who took the therapeutic posture presented by the Freudians to an extreme. He magnified the detached, dispassionate posture developed by the followers of Ego psychology. In his recorded lectures he defines his mission as helping people build Ego strength through the development of strong boundaries.[17] He believes therapists should offer themselves as models of self-control with which their clients can identify. The kind of therapeutic relationship which can best construct strong Ego boundaries, he tells us, is one that has well-defined boundaries itself. Langsians establish these boundaries with a set of firm, non-negotiable rules, such as a fixed fee and a consistent time and frequency for appointments. They even use sparse furnishings and a barren atmosphere to help define and regulate the relationship. They feel any compromise in the rules, which Langs defines as the frame, compromises the development of the client. Strict confidentiality hermetically seals the Langsian therapeutic container.

Langs analyzed the therapeutic relationship in minute detail. Remaining unwavering in his allegiance to distance and objectivity, he kept himself neutral, an unbiased clinical observer. From this position, he evaluated his own and his clients' responses with relentless scientific curiosity. In contrast to his emphasis on the importance of these distinct boundaries, the results of his research ultimately shortened the distance between client and therapist and supported the growth of feminine consciousness. Paradoxically, as for Freud, the empirical evidence of his systematic scientific inquiries became a means of reaching a more subjective reality. His conclusions, if understood in their fullest context, pushed therapy further into the quantum age. Like the quantum physicists, Langs unwittingly discovered a place in the relationship where there are no boundaries between therapist and client.

After many years of observation, he concluded that the healing that happens in therapy occurs largely as a result of the therapeutic relationship itself. The client's growth occurs within the context of the interaction between physician and patient. Langs calls this interaction the "bipersonal field" and describes it as a "fluctuating, shared creation of the patient and analyst."[18]

To translate his psycho-jargon into the language of the quantum physicists: the experimenter (psychotherapist) cannot study his object (patient) in isolation. The experimenter affects the experiment and is affected by it. Reality is created when the observed system interacts with the observing system. In Langsian terms, the outcome of therapy depends on an unconscious interactional process taking place between client and therapist.[19]

When Langs listened to the dialogue between client and therapist, he picked up clues about a different kind of conversation, one other than that which could be heard by the human ear. Apparently each person was constantly taking an intuitive psychic reading of the other. Although he may not have intended to, Langs described a relationship between client and therapist that is just like the relationship among those photons mentioned in the double-slit experiment and among the cells of the corn plants in Barbara Mclintoc's experiments. Just as the photons instantaneously knew the whereabouts of their neighbors and the cells of the corn plant gave feedback to the DNA because they were interconnected, so the client and therapist are connected with one another. Each reads and reacts to the other's psychic messages, whether healthy or pathological.

In other words, Langs said that there is a communication between client and therapist that is not rational. It is intuitive. At this deeper level, the boundary between client and therapist disappears, proving for psychology the Taoist belief that,

> all of the things in our universe (including us) that appear to exist independently, are actually all part of the one, all-encompassing organic pattern, and that no parts of that pattern are ever really separate from it or each other.[20]

Langs stressed that these unconscious or implicit interactions between client and therapist are the "first order" work of therapy and should take precedence over consciously intended behavior because their effects are monumental.[21] Through them, analysts communicate implicitly their assumptions about the patient as well as the hidden aspects or their own personality. The patient "consistently, unconsciously monitors, perceives, and incorporates these aspects of the analyst behaviors. In addition to what they reveal about the analyst, they are an essential means through which the patient may come to distinguish...the analyst from past pathogenic figures, and the analytic interaction from past pathogenic interactions."[22] The patient hears both the analyst's conscious and unconscious communications. Therefore, discrepancies between the analysts' manifest intentions and their unconscious communications will evoke in the patient negative images of the analyst as hypocritical and confused. When analysts are unaware of their unconscious communication, they are in grave danger of undermining the therapeutic quality of the relationship.

According to Langs, client and therapist typically respond to these unspoken thoughts and unconscious complexes of the other in predictable ways. They will either attempt to fit themselves into the other's silent expectations, or they will reject them. In either case, it is a Catch-22 for clients. If clients succumb to the subtle pressure from the therapist to introject the therapist's assumptions about themselves, then clients swallow someone else's opinion and judgment. If, because of some internal strength, clients are able to reject the therapist's assumptions and spit them out, they will probably end up in a battle with the therapist. This battle will occur when therapists, if they are unaware of their own thoughts and complexes, sense their client's resistance, interpret it as a defense mechanism, and once again turn the problem back on the client.

Through these unconscious communications, the client accesses information about the therapist's pathology. Langs points out that the patient is "exquisitely sensitive to the therapist...."[23] Sometimes patients will use this information to exploit their therapists, but most often they will use it to try and cure them. Patients frequently meet great resistance from the unaware therapist either way.

With Langs' expanded definition of the therapeutic relationship, each partner now has to take responsibility for their effect on the other. Therapists must look differently at the information they receive from their own and their clients' projections. These internal messages are no longer something to be recognized and dispensed with. They are a very important means of communication and an instrument for healing.

Even with all our scientific lineage and all the effort psychotherapy has made to separate client and therapist, therapists are now beginning to understand this separation as an illusion after all. With the knowledge that these potent interchanges are going on beneath the boundaried, superficial reality of the therapeutic relationship as it is traditionally defined comes a demand for more awareness and accountability. Therapists must look carefully at what they are unconsciously communicating to their clients. Clients must raise their consciousness and ask what they are introjecting. What opinions and beliefs—with which they really don't agree—are they adapting from their therapists?

Given this realization of the significance of unconscious communication, it is of utmost importance to uncover exactly what the therapeutic posture which emerged from the priest/doctor tradition is communicating to its clients. What message does it unconsciously send with its objectivity and distance? What is implicit in the way its interaction is structured?

Therapists are undoubtedly communicating much about themselves with their acceptance of the power-over position. The way they cling to their firm and rigid boundaries may say more about their own needs than it does about the client's. Their refusal to have a more personal relationship with their clients may have more to do with their own lack of skill at relationship than it does with concern for protecting the client. Within the present structure, clients can either introject the therapist's message that they are helpless; confront the therapist, asking why he/she needs to be in power position; or leave therapy.

Being cognizant of the history of relationship and how the therapeutic relationship has developed out of this history brings into question the continuing validity of the assumptions underlying the classic Ego psychology paradigm. Is a stronger, more separate Ego identity still the most viable goal for therapy? Is it still true that the more separate the Ego, the stronger? In many cases, the more distanced and less personal therapists are, the less healing the therapeutic encounter will be. Rigid boundaries and a fixed "frame" can actually compromise the client's development.

Considering the implications of therapists' unconscious communication with their clients: What are the effects on the client of the power-over relationship? Does confession taken from a position of authority really heal? What really happens when clients reveal their most personal life to an unrevealing therapist? Is cognitive insight still enough to heal? Is the priest/doctor posture still relevant? Langs tells us the most critical moment of therapy occurs at the instant when the therapist acts differently from past pathogenic illness-causing encounters, "giving the client a new experience."[24] What were our past pathogenic experiences and what is the new and healing experience we all need?

The authoritarian, power-over relationship is our pathogenic experience and the cause of many of today's emotional problems and suffering. The traditional structure of the doctor-patient or therapist-patient relationship increases our generation's psychological problems. The healing experience we need today is a relationship based on mutual respect and reciprocity, a relationship based on personal power, not power-over.

IV.
THE NEXT STEP

THE CREATIVE and THE RECEPTIVE. In the last analysis, this cannot be called a dualism. The two principles are united by a relation based on homogeneity; they do not combat but compliment each other. The difference in level creates a potential, as it were, by virtue of which movement and living expression of energy become possible.[1]

All truth is relative and the process of evolution is open-ended. In this process the advances of the past create the conundrum of the future. Western civilization has progressed from self-caused problem to self-caused problem. We suffer today from the effects of yesterday's antidote. From the transcendent height of their masculine stance, our predecessors could not see the damage they were doing. The wounded feminine soul awaited the breath of life from the spirit. It is just now that these two separate parts of the human being are finally recognizing one another, saying quietly to each other, "I need you for we are actually one."

Western people are just beginning to relate to woman as real. She is cowering in the corner, covering her shame, drenched in rage, turned inward against herself. Looking at her now, we cannot keep the distance we once had. We actually feel her shame and anger, and we should—because it is our own.

Only because we are connecting with her and her experience has become ours are we now able to see the damage caused by the coldness and rigidity with which the male hierarchy established and maintained its authority. We are beginning to acknowledge the ache deep within, which our predecessors could not feel from their inured distance.

Our predecessors caused the pathologies of today by their obsession with domination and their insistence on an identity limited to Ego. Keller tells us our current psychological pathologies are the result of "a preoccupation with superiority and inferiority, and the equation of self-esteem with a position in the power hierarchy."[2] She uses sadomasochism and paranoia as examples to reveal the pathological results of our historical separation from ourselves and each other. Sadomasochism is the achievement of pleasure from domination or subordination. Paranoia is our fear of our own attraction to this domination or subordination. Those of us who have experienced the pleasure of putting someone in checkmate or have enjoyed the sweetness of revenge know how thin and frail our compassion can be. Those of us who know the relief of letting someone else be responsible understand how vulnerable we are to the power-over relationship.

When we study the shifts in the therapeutic relationship over time, it appears therapists began to make changes as they were needed without fully understanding they had done so. Beginning with Freud, therapists have headed in a direction of healing the wounded feminine. As therapists leaned into the turn, they changed their position to balance their needs and those of their clients. Let's follow the course of our society's therapy and discover how these changes took place. We will also see where and how we are blocked in the process of fully integrating feminine consciousness into the therapeutic relationship.

The silent Freudian analysts were a blank screen. In their efforts to relate to someone, and not being given a clue about the person in the opposite chair, clients projected their own reactions and feelings onto the therapist. The therapist reflected these feelings and reactions back to the client, illuminating so much that had previously been unconscious. Clients then had to own these feelings and reactions as their own. With this owning, the evolutionary process took a large step forward. But, successfully completing their Freudian analysis, clients looked at the other chair and realized it was empty. They now knew much more about themselves but needed someone to be there with them and fully accept them.

Freud's position relative to his client's traced its authority back through science and the Judeo-Christian tradition. But gradually, in response to both the client's and the therapist's need for relationship, therapists began to move out from under the enormous weight of these social structures. Fortunately, their incorrigible propensity to take care of their clients' needs motivated therapists to break the rules. As much as they tried to follow the rules with a compliance brought about by the fear of professional disgrace; as frightened as they were of the consequences for themselves and their clients should their experiment fail, slowly therapists began to change their relationship with their clients.

Humanist therapy, as exemplified by Carl Rogers, met this need and validated the client's emotional experience. With its acceptance of the client's reality and its basic tenet of unconditional positive regard, Rogerians relieved the clients' sense of inferiority and feelings of shame.[10] Through the eyes of this new therapist, who genuinely felt this regard, clients began to love the selves that they had only recently owned. This was the second landmark occurrence in our society's progression toward the integration of feminine consciousness. Now clients not only knew themselves but could begin to love themselves. When they completed therapy with Rogers, they looked over in the other chair and saw acceptance and understanding sitting there. Clients appreciated this but still felt alone. What was missing was the possibility for the clients' expression of love. Freud helped clients become aware of much of the personal history they had kept hidden from themselves. Rogers and the humanists helped clients accept and integrate these memories. Now clients were looking for more.

So, continuing to follow their urge toward wholeness, clients made an appointment with Robert Langs or Sheldon Kopp. Although these therapists still restrained themselves from the "gratification" of giving their clients a full person with whom they could relate, they were aware, at least, that relationship is a significant part of therapy. They acknowledged that the therapeutic relationship involved mutual influence and reciprocity.

Kopp freely talked about the changes he went through during his years of sitting in the therapist's chair. At first he saw himself as a "guardian angel, a Moses." Then, he moved from this "arrogantly presumptuous" position to mock humility and fancied himself a saint. Finally he settled on a karmic understanding of the interaction, one which acknowledged a mutual responsibility.[3]

Now the therapist was beginning to take some form and shape, but this new personal stance had its limit. When clients leaned forward to connect, the therapist was still elusive. He disappeared like a mirage into the safe confines of the old Freudian therapeutic container, insisting on "maintaining the therapeutic posture of anonymity to the end."[4] When clients said "Hello" to the therapist on the elevator, they got no response. The therapist believed a personal or social interaction would break the therapeutic container and contaminate the therapy.

When clients pointed out the contradiction—therapists on the one hand saying a relationship of mutual influence is what makes therapy healing, and on the other hand displaying an unwillingness to enter into that relationship—therapists dug in their heels and became even more firm. Then clients reminded their therapists of the words they had told their clients, "It is our job to find out that [we] defend ourselves, then by what means, and finally against what."[5] Clients had a sudden insight: Therapists were using firm boundaries to deal with their fear. They were defending themselves against a personal relationship with the client. Therapists had reached their limit but could not acknowledge that it was *their* limit, not the client's.

A developmental lag was operative. Therapists were unable to see that the obvious answer to this contradiction was to change the unequal distribution of power in the therapeutic relationship. Keller reminds us that scientists experienced a similar developmental lag when the discoveries of quantum physics contradicted their traditional beliefs. She explains their unwillingness or inability to integrate the conflicting information using the developmental paradigm of the noted developmental psychologist Jean Claude Piaget. These scientists and therapists were in the throes of what Piaget calls cognitive repression.

Piaget describes cognitive repression as occurring at a stage in child development when children acquire a new understanding which conflicts with their old cognitive structures.[6] The child at this stage can hold two contradictory beliefs and will answer questions in contradictory ways, much as these therapists were doing. "Is it a relationship of reciprocity and mutuality that makes therapy healing?" "Yes, certainly!" these therapists said confidently. "Are you willing to reveal yourself in a personal encounter with your clients?" "Oh no," they answered, naively unaware of the contradiction. When faced with the glitch in logic, these therapists acted the same way the children Piaget studied did. They became defensive and confused, and they denied and avoided.

So, growing more than a bit weary, but with admirable perseverance, the clients sat in the waiting room of yet another therapist. The clients' eyes were drawn to a picture on the wall. It depicted a sleek black Annubus who, with deep unfeeling eyes, communicated its readiness to guide them to the underworld. When they entered the consulting room, they found themselves sitting opposite a Jungian analyst. This therapist was able to guide clients past their personal history into the deepest regions of the unconscious. The Jungian analyst led them into this unknown part of themselves which the analyst called the feminine soul. Through the process of therapy, clients resurrected the feminine consciousness which had long been buried beneath the layers of the male power structure.

When clients had begun their treatment with Dr. Freud, they told him they were being abused and neglected. They told him they had been and were still being traumatized and raped. Apparently, with tremendous conscientiousness and perseverance against strong impulses to the contrary, the Freudian therapist had kept a safe distance from clients. Using theory to create this distance, the therapist managed to avoid physically traumatizing them again. Now, after many stops in between, clients sat in front of a person who acknowledged that fathers actually rape their daughters. This person understood the daughter's hysteria as a flashback to that rape. The analyst realized that the rape of the feminine was embodied in Freud's very idea that rape could be a wish-fulfilling fantasy. He/she knew that the abuse had been systematic and that it was both literal and symbolic because it happened to the psyche as well as to the body. This Jungian analyst saw clearly that the therapist had been involved in perpetuating the figurative and actual violation of the feminine in their patients.

The clients and their new therapist set about accomplishing the Piagetian task of cognitive restructuring, finding a solution to the cognitive repression. This analyst, like the Zen masters of physics and biology, realized that the process of intensifying conflict would yield a new and larger consciousness. So their first priority was to restore and strengthen the feminine, giving her voice and form. When clients did this, they could really hear, see, and feel the conflict with the overextended masculine. The stronger the voice of the feminine, the clearer the conflict became. The Jungian analyst knew that lifting the feminine out of its repressed position broke the rules laid down by the masculine authority. He/she realized the driving need for connection and that the judgment against it caused pathology and pain.

With the understanding that clients needed to suffer the most complete agony of the conflict in order to reach a greater understanding, the Jungian analyst guided them into the realm of archetype and myth. Here clients actually felt in themselves the power of Yahweh, the holiness of the priest and the pure brilliance of the scientific hero, the man of reason. Clients also identified with the Goddess, crushed and humiliated, whom they now exhumed from the ruins of a lost civilization. They found the place in themselves that was the spirit. They resonated with the ariel hum of angels from somewhere above, longing for transcendence, knowing the earth was not their home. But the Jungian therapist wouldn't let them stay at that transcendent height. Reminiscent of the priestess in the dream at the beginning of the "Therapy" chapter, the therapist beat the primitive ritual drum that quickened the loins. Then the clients were brought down from their heady heights and began to dance in rhythm with the earth and be warmed by the heat of their fellow dancers.

This was soul, Eros, the opposite of distance. Clients experienced and felt. They suffered the passion. It became obvious why people had defended against it. Clients now actually felt the agony of Christ in the first person—not symbolically, not detached. They were suspended on the cross, fully feeling what was taking place. They were nailed to it by soul, by their involvement in life, and by their human limitations. In agony they strained against these limits, reaching toward the perfection they desired.

Clients were frightened. They sensed they had barely tapped into these awesome energies. Where would these energies take them? The therapists, even with all their trust in the process, were frightened too. Just when clients felt the most lost and abandoned and questioned why they had started the journey, it happened—the shift the Jungian therapist promised would occur as a result of heightening the conflict between masculine and feminine. The whole became larger than the sum of its parts. Clients stood above the conflict and surrendered to its lesson. Then they understood that they could not possibly maintain peace between the powerful forces of archetypal masculine spirit and feminine soul. It had been foolish of them to imagine that they could contain the passions of the gods and goddesses with the paltry willpower of their little Egos. Clearly, their Egos were not in command.

When the Ego relinquished its position as central authority, clients gave up their hope for control, realizing this hope was naive. Then they waited for the disaster their former therapists had warned would happen. However, they discovered that this surrender did not result in the annihilation they thought it would. They found, to their great surprise and relief, that their Ego survived the admission that its control was an illusion. From this new perspective, clients understood that they had behaved like over-responsible children, depressed by their failures and anxious because of their limitations. Now they were gratefully relieved of a job that had always been too big for them.

The clients' perseverance in the painful holding of the opposites of body and mind, soul and spirit—refusing to relinquish either—forced them into a larger consciousness. Their new consciousness incorporated both separateness and connection, individuality and relatedness. Soul contained spirit, giving it form. In the new reality, they understood that opposition itself was a function of relatedness.

This is where the client is now. Their work with their Jungian therapist is not complete. However, they have permeated the walls containing the Ego and have traveled through them to an expanded identity. This identity is larger than their tiny Ego selves. It includes the reality of other voices and visions. Now clients are accomplishing the true goal of science. Finally, they truly are the observers. However, their experience is very different. Now they can take the role of observer but without objectifying, because what they are observing is subjective. It is themselves.

When clients begin to process this experience of connection through their thinking function, their Egos ask the logical questions, "Who is this observer? Whose experience is this? Whose reality?" Then their minds take the cognitive leap their experience took. They realize on a logical level that there exists a much larger Self than they had known. Their minds deduce the answer, "It must be the eyes and experience of the Deity!"

Clients haven't yet fully programmed their experience onto the software of their rational minds. They know, with a feminine knowing, psychically, emotionally, and kinesthetically, the thrill of relinquishing control, dissolving boundaries, surrendering to a higher power. They also know through their own experience it is possible to give up control without being annihilated. But they are just now restructuring their cognitions and behavior to fit their experience. The far-reaching implications of the boundariless experience are just dawning on them.

When clients translate this change in perspective from an archetypal to a personal level, they find that not only are they in a different relationship with the Deity, but with other human beings as well. Through the Deity's eyes, their neighbors look different. People's efforts to control and dominate one another, as though they are separate, becomes ludicrous. Out of this experience, they must write a new definition for power and strength and set new goals for their relationships. The clients' goal now is to know their own reality and the realities of other people as well—those of all sentient beings, neighbors, families, and their therapist. They must now redefine power and strength as the ability to traverse these realities and to maintain an awareness of the overriding oneness. Therapists and clients must shake themselves awake and catch up.

They must connect what they know in their hearts to be right action with their rational beliefs and their behavior in the therapeutic relationship.

In order to do this, both participants in the therapeutic relationship must understand and own their relationship with power. History has placed both therapist and client in a situation where there is an unequal distribution of power. When therapists open their office doors and invite clients in to have a seat, the stage is already set. As the play unfolds, they find themselves in a period piece. The playwright and the director have placed them in a situation where there is an unequal distribution of power. The backdrop, props, and dialogue all support this dynamic.

Both client and therapist must be brutally honest about their own relationship with power. Therapists must ask themselves, "Are there times I actually enjoy having power over the client? Intentionally or unintentionally, do I encourage the person in the opposite chair to remain a 'patient' so that I can feel superior? At times, out of my insecurities or out of habit, do I promote the client's weakness?"

Clients must mirror these questions: "Are there times when I actually want the therapist to have the answers for me? Do I encourage the person in the opposite chair to take responsibility for my life? Do I, out of my own insecurities or out of habit, support the therapist's omnipotence?"

Therapists must be aware of another scenario of the power dynamic. If the therapists themselves have ever been abused by power, they will tend to have a reaction formation against it and back away from it. They may want to disown that they have any power in the relationship at all. "I do not have or want power in this relationship," they say to themselves because they think power itself is what is dangerous. They want the relationship to be equal and think this can be accomplished if they relinquish all power. But this denial of power by the therapist is as dangerous as the assumption of the power-over position.

When therapists deny their power, they are misinterpreting the meaning of power and equality because they are caught in the old way of thinking. "Personal power" and "power-over" are very different things. Therapists must own their personal power. Out of their learned fear of power, they also misinterpret equality. When thinking "power" means "power over," they think in an equal relationship neither person should have any power. This is not true. Equality means recognizing that both people have power.

Because of their reaction formation to the abuse of power, therapists can hurt clients by disavowing the position they are in and the potent impact they have. If they don't own this impact, they will lose their greatest strength: the ability to hear the dialogue of mutual influence. Therapists must not simply disown all of their power now out of fear of abusing it.

When therapists understand the nature of the power dynamic in the therapeutic relationship, they may find they can best serve their clients as coaches and guides. They can teach clients about this power dynamic and lead them into a relationship with them that is symmetrical. But remember, the guide must make the journey. Therapists have only themselves to use as tools. They must be able to stretch their boundaries enough to confirm their clients' reality. Then they can help clients to strengthen their boundaries. By offering a genuine relationship, they can entice clients to stretch their boundaries to their limit and a little beyond in order to join the therapist in a relationship. Then the therapist can sensitively allow the client to retract their boundary again in rhythm with their own needs. Repeating this exercise makes boundaries stronger and more flexible.

With grace, client and therapist might be able to travel together to the place where both can see through the eyes of the reality they create in relationship together. When their Egos become strong enough to risk it, they might even be able to dissolve all boundaries between them and revisit a state of oneness.

Therapists have to make the journey. They can't just repeat words without risking the experience. Unless they really develop a relationship with their clients, they will come across as over-intellectualized, arrogant, and irritating. Giving the answers from an acquired place will not work. "We're equal because it's all one," therapists could glibly tell their clients. Intellectually they may know that as truth, but without the experience of sharing a reality, it is meaningless. Equality and oneness is an experience, discovered through a process. It is not a thought.

If therapists are too stiff and rigid, they won't be able to make this journey with their clients. They will be left like old folks in their rockers, sitting on the front porch, watching those who are more flexible walk into the future.

Therapists have to be willing to risk more intimacy, and in so doing be more vulnerable. It is only through risking vulnerability that people grow. Growth occurs when security falls back, exposing the hidden, soft places where the role thins out and exposes nakedness. Therapists need to expose themselves, allowing their clients to see them as they really are. They must stop pulling their role around them for protection.

In *Power in the Helping Professions*, a Jungian analyst, Adolf Guggenbuhl Craig, tells us what his teacher, Carl Jung, said therapists need in order to stop violating their clients. "Only through emotional interchange with those to whom he [the therapist] stands in a relation of love can a needed dimension be brought in his benumbed world."[7] Craig himself realizes that the scientific approach of the therapist "coolly and objectively tracking down the destructiveness in his patients" doesn't heal any longer.[8] He knows the only thing that will save the therapist from what he calls the power shadow is a "loving, but forceful encounter with equals."[9]

Here, however, he enters into that now-familiar Piagetian repression. Craig knows that "a psychotherapist who succeeds in avoiding the pitfalls of the rigidifying split can perform an incalculable service for humanity."[10] He even continues with the strong statement, "In my opinion, and on the basis of my experience, there is only one thing which can ameliorate or even dissolve the therapist's shadow-entanglement: friendship."[11] But when he takes this line of thinking to its logical conclusion—"What the analyst needs [in order to heal the power shadow] is symmetrical relationships"[12]—he is not able to make the obvious connection to a symmetrical relationship with clients. Even though he knows that it is Eros, relationship, that is needed to heal in our time, he was not able to separate himself from the operative cultural assumptions about the nature of the relationship between client and therapist.

Craig is stuck in a cultural belief which he believes to be carved in stone. The client and the therapist are not equal. For Craig, apparently the client is not a "real person," capable or worthy of the kind of relationship that eliminates the power shadow. He believes that by definition the therapeutic relationship must be asymmetrical. This is the setup as it has been handed down to us by history. It is codified in state laws and ethical standards regulating the profession. But therapists need to question this basic assumption. Otherwise, like the Freudians did when they denied their patients' reality, therapists will violate their clients by not recognizing them as full human beings. They prevent the relationship from being a healing one by their narrow interpretation of adherence to an old form. As long as they hold on to it, therapists will hurt their clients instead of help.

If clients and therapists are going to have this kind of reciprocal relationship, and if they are not going to follow the old rules, then how will they establish boundaries? How will they know what kind of boundaries each relationship needs? The answer lies within the concept of reciprocity. Like Mclintoc's corn plant and its DNA had a mutual feedback system, clients and therapists will give and receive feedback with one another. They will have to listen to each other with all the skill and knowledge they each have. Each must attend to the power dynamic; each must try to help the other increase his/her awareness of the influence that dynamic has in the relationship. Each will encourage the other to investigate what kind of boundaries each needs to have and to tell the other when one is too close or not close enough. Both must use all of their soul-searching ability to know their own motives.

Counselors and clients have come a long way from the days when their final goal was only independence and autonomy. Now they also have the job of encouraging relationship. This is a much more difficult, complicated, and delicate task than the one before. They are all new at it, and they will make mistakes. They will pray that none of these mistakes harms either of them—client or counselor. The more both participants surrender to their imperfections and allow a genuine level of involvement, the more potential there will be for growth. As therapists and clients grow together, they will both become more adept.

Clients and therapists need to be free to set the kind of boundaries each individual relationship demands. Therapists are less likely to hurt clients from this position than they were when they accepted the power-over relationship as an imperative. Because therapists are receptive to the conscious and unconscious communication in the therapeutic relationship, they will be able to respond more appropriately to their clients. They will hear some clients say, "I need you to have clearly defined boundaries because I am still developing mine, and this gives me the safety to do so." Other clients will tell their therapists that a highly structured relationship is stifling for them. Counselors will answer according to what they can handle. Sometimes they will be afraid to meet the client where the client needs them to. Or sometimes the therapist will be willing but just not ready to. Each client comes to therapy with a different consciousness and different needs. Therapists must ask permission to enter the client's space and in turn invite the client into theirs when the time is right. Both counselor and client must acknowledge what they know and what the other knows. Using all of the awareness they can muster, they will facilitate the process of healing. Working in reciprocity, they will create a relationship.

The therapist is still a therapist, but now working in an expanded therapeutic container. This involves more choices and more response-ability. It means therapists must sometimes risk being seen in all their humanness. But isn't that what therapists want the client to know and value in themselves? By the end of therapy, clients will no longer see therapists as having power over them. Both partners will be moving together in an interpretive dance. The relationship, no longer a minuet or foxtrot, does not follow a prescribed pattern with one person always assuming the lead. In this new dance, the lead shifts and is often indistinguishable as the partners move in relationship to one another. They move and change in rhythm with each other: now the therapists leads, now the client, now both. The dance, the boundary, the relationship evolves. Nothing is permanent. It all changes. They have become partners in healing.

> This world of the immutable is the daemonic world, in which there is no free choice, in which everything is fixed. It is the world of yin. But in addition to this rigid world of number, there are living trends. Things develop, consolidate in a given direction, grow rigid, then decline; change sets in, coherence is maintained. He who succeeds in endowing his work with this regenerative power creates something organic, and the thing so created is enduring. [13]

V.
SETTING BOUNDARIES

Let us sit in silence, freeing ourselves from all conditioning. Let us take away the mask that we have found convenient to move in the crowds, the image that people expect us to fulfill. May we face ourselves and face the world and face each being, with deep insight of the Divine Consciousness untrammeled by the individual ego, that life may become meaningful and that our purpose may be fulfilled.[1]

I see you therapists and clients nodding in agreement, allowing the cloak of your traditional roles to loosen around you. You agree that we need to be free to set boundaries as the individual therapeutic interaction demands. You value reciprocity and are willing to promote dialogue and encourage relationship. The idea of risking more intimacy seems right. I can see you unwrapping the old cloak, ready to step out of it; then you hesitate, poised on the brink of change. Part of you is still uncomfortable and resists.

Let's honor that resistance for the moment. Turn your ear toward the reticent voice within. Ask it what is making it uncomfortable. "All well and good," the reticent voice answers, "but, first of all, are therapists to throw away all of their training and vilify all of the master therapists? And secondly," it goes on, having apparently given this question a great deal of thought, "I need to know in more concrete terms how therapists and clients are going to make boundary decisions in their new authentic relationship." The reticent voice is clear about what it needs in order to be prepared to leave the old role behind and take the journey into the unknown. It doesn't mind trailblazing, but it wants to have all of the right equipment.

Resistance speaks with a practical voice. In its wisdom it demands a good map and a true compass. It remembers why therapists established their firm boundaries to begin with and why society passed laws to preserve them. And it reminds therapists about the fear of clients being abused or exploited. This hesitation in the face of change comes out of conscientiousness and a sincere desire to heal. Therapists have too much at stake to risk flying by the seat of their pants. If they aren't comfortable making these boundary decisions, and they won't leave the old role behind until they are.

Realizing how overextended masculine consciousness has become does not mean throwing it away
completely. In fact, this "all or nothing" thinking is just
the problem. If it's not all structure and rationality,
then we therapists fear it will be all intuition—and a
foggy intuition at that, unperfected and untrustworthy.
No wonder we're reticent and uncomfortable. Archae-
ologists used to think that in the old matriarchal cultures women ruled. They were making assumptions
from the sclerosed masculine perspective that someone
must rule, if not men then women. Actually, as the
more modern archaeologist Marija Gimbutas' discoveries prove, this was not the case. The recently excavated
ruins of the matriarchal Minoan civilization of Crete
clearly prove that, in fact, these feminine cultures were
egalitarian. No one ruled.[2]

As we resurrect the lost feminine perspective and
recognize its relevance for the therapeutic relationship,
we can come more into balance. The reticent voice will
be relieved to know we are not going to throw away all
of our theories. We will make good boundary decisions
by using all of our knowledge as well as developing our
intuition into a trusted ally.

There is a way to use theory which makes it most
helpful in making boundary decisions. We therapists
can glean a great deal from our academic knowledge
through understanding it from a developmental perspective. Then we will not get caught in the smaller
perspective, the one of the moment. Focusing on the
perspective of the moment gets us stuck by allowing us
to believe that what we think now is the ultimate truth
and that our deductions from this truth are infallible.
This makes past beliefs appear stupid and prohibits
future growth. With a focus on the historical sequence,

the theories each of the vanguard therapists high-lighted earlier characterize an evolutionary moment. By bringing this moment into their society's awareness, they made conscious something previously uncon-scious. In so doing, they became catalysts for change. Each of the major theorists have contributed to the development of our present consciousness.

The theories of the vanguard therapists each pro-vided a bridge from a smaller, more rigid definition of Self to an expanded, more flexible Self. Each such change required a challenging reorganization of iden-tity. These therapists provided creative moments for the individuals with whom they worked, and their theories provided a creative moment for the larger society. Evolution is made up of many steps of increas-ing "I"-ness.[3]

If we overlook the deficiencies and misconceptions caused by the limitations of their understanding, we find that each therapist took the stance of a larger Self. They modeled that which the client needed to integrate in order to grow. Their theories described society's evolutionary and the individual's developmental situa-tion. Each therapist exemplified an individual and collective stage by their definition of the Self and its boundaries. They told us how to recognize these stages by describing the typical growing pains, conflicts and tensions, and by defining the developmental tasks demanded for that particular transition. By seeing the larger more general patterns and direction and not getting lost in the differences and details, we notice a developmental sequence. If we don't make obstacles of ourselves by clinging to our current perspective and secure definitions, we can free ourselves to utilize a variety of theories and techniques when they are relevant for our clients. In so doing we gain access to a wide base of knowledge.

The way in which these vanguard therapists interacted with their clients—whether observing silently, empathetically, or transpersonally—is illustrative of the evolving structure of relationship in our society as a whole. On an individual level, their interaction with their clients delineated changes in both interpersonal and interpsychic boundaries. It described the changes taking place in the boundary between Self and others and changes taking place in the relationship of the individual parts of the personality to the whole personality.

Let's look again at three vanguard therapeutic models to help understand the specific developmental tasks these evolutionary changes demanded. How did therapists encourage the stretching of identity and relationship boundaries? How did they describe the conflicts and tensions of that stretch? What was the developmental task each of these therapists addressed? Using the Freudian analytic stance, the Rogerian humanist perspective, and the Jungian transpersonal model, we can track the growth and change in psychotherapy. Freud described and catalyzed society's movement from a mutable world of sensations to a coherent definition of Self and identity. While his contemporaries kept their focus on tracking an ever-changing world of sensations and the structural sense organs of perception, he pursued the invisible integrating force, the "I," who was the stable entity in a moving world of phenomena.

With his lyrical description of the internal psyche, Freud depicted a drama. The main character, whose conflicts and passions we can easily recognize in our clients, is trying to develop an integrated identity or Ego. Using this Freudian description, it is possible to assess where clients are in the drama of identity development. Freud explains what needs to be done if we see a client in the throes of his or her Id, lusty and untamed, or a client who is one with his or her body and its energy and cannot discriminate between his or her outer and inner world. If the client is gratified by dream images, fantasy, and external reality indiscriminately, and is alternately in a luscious or agonizing whirl of desires, fulfillments, and disappointments, then we can use a Freudian stance and midwife the birth of the Ego.

When we see the birth of the tiny Ego in our clients, it grabs at our empathy. It is such a magical and conscientious youth. Not fully grown, it works as an agent of the Id. We watch it venture forth into the outside world. Using our understanding of Freudian psychology, we can help the young Ego in its struggle to discriminate between concrete reality and fantasy. When it succeeds and proudly brings a real apple to the Id, as opposed to the image of an apple, we applaud. Even if we attempt to maintain the neutral stance dictated by our analytic training, we can't help but be pleased by how smart the Ego is becoming. We encourage the client's Id to depend on Ego to negotiate for it in a world it doesn't understand. But this is a heavy burden for such a youngster. We worry if it's too much responsibility too soon. But the Ego is valiant and steadfast in its efforts to satisfy Id, and satisfying the Id is its major pleasure, until the entrance of the father, the Super Ego.

The Ego's father's demands are quite different from those of the Id. He requires of Ego that it separate from its beloved Id and develop a social conscience. There are now things the Ego is not supposed to do because Super Ego tells it they are improper or will hurt others. The Ego is now limited in the ways it can gratify Id. Father seems to have gotten his concept of right and wrong from some outside authority. Until its father's appearance, Ego didn't know there was any outside authority. The paternal Super Ego wields the power of society with a strong arm, using shame and guilt. He is powerful, and the Ego is both in awe of him and terrified by him. Soon the Ego begins to deny its attraction to lusty pleasures even to itself.

As we watch our clients go through this drama, we, like the Freudians, want to help them develop stronger identities and minds of their own. We can assist with this developmental task by using a Freudian approach modified by our historical understanding. We know, from our developmental perspective, that we want this young Ego to realize, with gradual insight, that if Super Ego can be separate from Id, then separation is possible. As we watch the Ego become tired of the conflicts between itself, Id, and Super Ego, we want to encourage it to detach from both of them. We want, as Freud did, to help it gain strength and develop its own identity, its own preferences. It is time for it to leave home.

Using Freudian techniques tempered by experience, we move in to help the Ego. We pattern ourselves after Freud and proceed in the way all truly good therapists do. We model what it is we want our clients to become. At first we, as Freud taught us, are the neutral observer, allowing the client to believe the conflict is with us, projecting it, externalizing it. Then we act as the interpreter, feeding back to the client their projections as a map of their own internal conflict. We bring the

SETTING BOUNDARIES / 113

light of consciousness to the problems and conflicts by naming and describing them. We put boundaries around them and contain them. We try, as best we can, to remain neutral and not be father or mother, Super Ego or Id. We are the Ego's most loyal fan. We see and treat our client as a separate individual.

But Freud did not stop there. He taught us to have enough faith to push our client on toward a higher truth. Using his techniques for exposing defense mechanisms, we increase the tension of the conflict, demanding the Ego become stronger. We attack on two fronts. First we pull up personal history, memories that cause the Ego to shudder in fear of the reprisal, the punishment of Super Ego. Freud taught us to be relentless. We attack on a second front. Each time the Ego comes up with some ingenious way to defend itself from this personal history, we give the defense a name. We say, for example, that it is repression or denial, and with the naming of it, we expose it.

Freud listened to his clients talk without interruption. He listened to their dreams and to their associations. Because he seldom interrupted them, he began to realize that everything the client said was somehow related to the last thing they had said, even if the client was unconscious of the connection. From this and his sense of the energy surrounding a word, image, story, or dream, he found clues to unconscious material. He dug deeper, pulling up more repressed personal history, memories that did not fit with the client's self-image.

Then when his client tried to deflect from the situation by getting tied in knots with anxiety or acting out, he brought the light of consciousness to their response. And he kept naming and labeling these responses until there was no hiding. Back to the issue: This is who you are, what you think and feel, what you have done and what has been done to you. And these are your defenses against it.

In order to use Freudian techniques, modern therapists must be as soul-searching as he was. Like Freud we must courageously analyze ourselves, looking for the ripples on the smooth surface of our own psyche and diving in to find their cause. We must go through the same self-searching process through which we are leading our clients.

When the developmental task is that of forming a strong and stable identity, then a Freudian stance is often constructive. In order to help people define themselves, Freudians recommend that therapists maintain a firm self-boundary. Often the best thing we can do for clients who are at this stage of development is to be impenetrable. Their projections bounce off us, back to them. This is the time when it is more appropriate to be the impervious, observing "I." We must take care to own what is ours and only what is ours, throwing back to the clients only what belongs to them. We must take care neither to act from our own Id—needing gratification and pleasure from our clients, even at their expense—nor from our own Super Ego, expounding our judgments of rights and wrongs. These are times when we can help our clients define their reality with our own firm self-definition and solid boundaries.

We need to encourage the client to be as powerful as we are, to butt up against us with their own firm identity boundaries. They must only accept what belongs to them and give back to us what belongs to us. Our goal is to have a partner who is as strong as we are. We encourage their self-assertion against us. In

The Symbolic Quest, Edward Whitmont says, "A basic test of ego development is the ability to assert one's own will in the face of opposition and resistance, and to exert one's drive for power."[4] Our clients discover their power in relationship to ours. By separating from us, our clients start to know themselves. Freud was admittedly limited by the era in which he lived, but we would do well to be as creative and courageous an explorer as he. With our historical perspective, we have the advantage. We know the rest of the story. With what is now hindsight for us, we don't have to get lost in thinking that all life is about reducing the tensions between instincts and conscience, nor is developing a strong Ego identity the final goal.

Today we don't have to be quite so afraid of the Id. Our Super Egos don't have to be quite so rigid as to see all instincts as antisocial and regressive. We know all is not worry and illness. We can take the best of Freud and see him as a pioneer. His was the first developmental paradigm, and he was the first to venture into the unconscious. His theory also contained, however immature and rigid, the beginnings of a social conscience.

Theorists who carried on the Freudian tradition called themselves Ego psychologists. They laid out a developmental sequence from infancy to old age. Primary in this linear model was the development of the Ego. To a large extent, they saw human development as synonymous with Ego development. They further expanded the role and function of the Ego. The Ego psychologists said that in order for the Ego to be more sound, vigorous, and creative in dealing with life, it must integrate the feelings and memories Freud helped to uncover. The neutral analytic stance, as good as it was for self-definition, would not help with this next developmental task. What was needed, at that point, was a more responsive and accepting therapist. At this stage of development, clients required a relationship which gave them an opportunity for self-expression and a sense of being acceptable. Carl Rogers and humanist theorists appeared just in time to role-model this kind of relationship. These humanists expanded the boundaries of the therapeutic relationship in a way their predecessors could not.

Rogers tuned in to the client's need for self-acceptance. He related from his heart, not from his head alone, not like "a physician expecting to diagnose and cure,—but as a person to a person."[5] He didn't focus on analysis, but instead on integrating what the Ego psychologists had unearthed. When our clients are filled with shame, blocking the flow of their energy, it is Rogerian boundaries we need to emulate. When they have delved into the shadowy unconscious and illuminated memories of abuse done to them and of abuse they have committed, they need to experience unconditional positive regard in order to integrate these memories into their identity. When they speak of incest or alcoholism or any of the dysfunctional things that went on beneath the surface of their post-Victorian homes, we need to give them Rogerian empathetic understanding. We, as therapists, must take down the rigid barriers that separate us from our clients and offer them our unconditional positive regard and empathetic understanding. We need to have trust in their potential for growth.

The humanistic approach, as exemplified by Rogers, demands that therapists use their intuition and their ability to go beyond the boundaries of their individual selves. To experience the reality of the client, therapists must call on an ability they have (or can develop) to truly be the other person for a moment. This is the experience of the feminine, Eros, our capacity to connect. Rogers says we should relate to our clients from a place of boundary diffusion, where "no inner barriers keep [us] from sensing what it feels like to be the client at each moment of the relationship."[6]

In order to help our clients through shame, guilt, and remorse we, like Rogers, must believe that "under certain conditions, involving primarily complete absence of any threat to the self-structure, experiences which are inconsistent with it may be perceived, and examined, and the structure of the Self revised to assimilate and include such experiences."[7] As therapists we must accept and integrate our own history with love and understanding if we are to serve as role models for our clients. When we have experienced the relief from inner tensions that results from accepting our past without judgment and assimilating more of ourselves, we will be able to help our clients do the same.

As we and our clients relax our internal boundaries and take a good look at our impulses in the light of consciousness, we see that many of these impulses are not as anti-social as Freud believed them to be. Buried along with the material that shamed us are strong impulses for relationship and feelings of caring. We find we are not so conflicted between impulse gratification and social conscience as we feared we would be. When we look at our impulses, we begin to see that some of our strongest impulses are for compassion and caring about and needing others.

If we as counselors are going through this healing experience ourselves, we well know that growth is self-motivated. Thus we can relinquish control of our clients. This is similar to the experience of parents when they realize their child does not *want* to get hurt on the playground and they give them more freedom. The role of protector is infantilizing; we must realize our clients are individuals capable of protecting themselves. The reciprocity of the relationship grows as our own boundaries become less rigid and we are more responsive to our clients. Only as our own self-image grows and our boundaries loosen are we able to help others to heal. We are healed in the process of healing. We become less rigid and more open to our own emotion. As Rogers would say, "The self-image begins to come closer to the real self."

We have utilized the feminine skills of empathy and compassion to help our clients. We have enabled them to take a step away from cause-and-effect thinking. Their past does not have to determine their future when they understand it, accept it, and integrate it. Still, as therapists, we are giving, but not revealing. Our focus has been on melting the defenses with which the frightened Ego protected itself. We can better understand and appreciate the client's struggle when we have experienced it ourselves. Then we know that for people to be seen and appreciated with all their humanness and evolutionary primitive past brings great relief.

As therapists we have met the evolutionary and developmental challenge and helped the client to remove the thick layer of defensive protection with our acceptance and unconditional positive regard, our love and compassion. We have helped clients solve the problem of identity confusion which Ego psychologists and humanists described by loosening our boundaries and accepting a bit of the feminine. We have helped reorganize and redefine the concept of Self. Less over-blown and unrealistic about what we must be in order to be okay, we no longer have to impersonate. Clients can be genuine and authentic because they accept our inconsistencies.

The clients feel great. They have moved out on their own. They have an apartment and a good job. They no longer depend on their parents. When they come home from work and maybe a trip to the health club for a workout, or from the hospice where they volunteer on Thursday evenings, they turn on the home entertain-ment system and lie down to rest. But they become restless and begin to switch the remote control from channel to channel, finally turning it off. Lying there in a technical silence, they realize they are lonely and alienated. "What's the meaning of it all?" they say to themselves. They turn to their therapist for help with their existential agony.

At this point, as the therapists, in order to help clients understand and overcome their loneliness and alienation, we must change from the stance of the humanists to the stance of the Jungians. The healing this new therapeutic model offers is contact with the numinous, the sacred. The Jungian model is spiritual and as such can help clients discover the meaning and purpose of their lives. It is progressive, not only retro-spective. The client's entire life experience becomes meaningful when the past is explained in terms of a hopeful future goal.

Jung offered a new expanded definition of the Self and with it an expanded identity. As therapists it behooves us to adopt this new definition because we know by now that we must model what the client needs to become. To Jungians the Self and the Ego are no longer synonymous. As Jungians describe the structure of the psyche, the Ego is no longer at the center. It is the center of consciousness, but they explain that it is no longer the chief executive officer. The most powerful and influential system of the psyche, according to the Jungians, is the vast Collective Unconscious.

The Collective Unconscious is all that is not conscious to the Ego.

> "It holds possibilities which are blocked away from the conscious mind, for it has at its disposal all the subliminal contents, all those things which have been forgotten or overlooked, as well as the wisdom and experience of uncounted centuries, which are laid down in its archetypal origins."[8]

The Collective Unconscious of the Jungians holds the personal history the Freudians unearthed and the humanists helped to integrate. Yet to the Jungians, there is more—in fact everything more. Jung's Unconscious is not limited to personal history. It includes everything that is "not us." Contact with the Collective Unconscious is a religious experience in the purest sense of the term "religious," and as such can fulfill our clients' need for meaning. We sense we are part of an infinitely larger whole which is purposefully evolving, becoming. Edward Whitmont explains that this kind of experience comes from contact with,

> a dynamic agency or effect not caused by an arbitrary act of will. On the contrary, it seizes

and controls the human subject which is
always its victim rather that its creator. The
"numinosum"—whatever its cause may be—
is an experience of the subject independent
of his will.[9]

This transcendent contact alters consciousness.
Through this contact with the Collective Unconscious,
people discover the meaning of their lives. Listening
carefully to Whitmont, we realize it is not human will
which makes this experience happen. So how are we,
as therapists, to facilitate this experience for clients?

In order to move toward the goal of helping our
alienated clients contact the Collective Unconscious
and discover their place in the universe and meaning
of their lives, we therapists must again shift our boundaries. We must model a new identity, that which Jung
calls the "self." The new center of being lies between the
Ego and the Collective Unconscious. If we see this as
an uncomfortable demotion of the Ego, we are in trouble because our therapeutic position needs to change
from champion of the Ego to champion of the new "self."

Once we have stepped into our new role, we notice
the characters are different but the position of the "self"
is a familiar one. It is another position calling for
mediation and communication between the parts of the
psyche. Much as the Ego mediated between the Super
Ego and the Id, the "self" mediates between the Ego and
the Collective Unconscious. In our new role, we model
the "self," encouraging communication between all
parts of the psyche. Jungians tell us to be flexible as
therapists. Our job is to model a deep respect for all the
different components of the person. And we must

change hats according to Jung's theory of entropy, always bolstering the weakest component. By doing this we help create a fully differentiated psyche. We may champion the Ego and conscious life at one point. At another time we might facilitate conscience or instinctual needs and desires. We also teach the client how to tap the deep unconscious, the transpersonal. As Freudians we used the signs on the surface of consciousness, such as dreams and associations, to detect a well-defended history. As Jungians we now add the use of symbol, myth, and metaphor as messengers from the depths of the unconscious. We amplify these, trying to translate the valued messages they bring. Like witches reading images appearing in a magic mirror or upon the moonlit surface of a magic pond, we help the client use symbols to communicate with the transpersonal realms.

Jung defines the developmental task as movement toward wholeness, complete integration. He tells us this is the goal of therapy, but we must not expect to accomplish it. The Collective Unconscious, he says, is infinite. We as limited beings can never be conscious of all of it. The most the Ego can do is stay in relationship with it, which is the job of the "self." The tensions and growing pains clients will encounter in their new identity as "self" are those intrinsic to the relationship between the Ego, or small individual identity, and the Collective Unconscious. Growth is achieved, as it is in the Freudian model, through heightening differences. In fact, according to Jungians, the solution to the loneliness and alienation is born out of this conflict between Ego and Unconscious. We, as therapists, must work toward highlighting the contradictory component parts of the personality and then have faith that the solution will emerge. We hope our clients will transcend the conflict and reach a higher understanding—one that can contain the opposites.

We can help our clients with this developmental task by encouraging them to recognize and support each part of their psyche. We will need to shift back and forth, now enhancing the Ego, now acknowledging the Collective Unconscious. Then we can highlight the conflict that arises when the Ego does not want to surrender to the greater power of the Unconscious. Thus we model the "self" we want them to discover. This "self" recognizes and respects differences within the individual psyche. By interacting with and honoring all of the parts of their psyche, we will enable them to do the same.

Our therapeutic role is complex. As we help our clients reach toward the goal of individuation or wholeness, our most important tool is our own relationship with the Collective Unconscious. We must have developed or be in the process of developing a "self" with which we identify. This "self" mediates and keeps communication open between the our Ego and the vast and unlimited Unconscious. Because we are in the process or have completed the process, we will enable our clients to do the same.

Our next most important tool is our relationship with the client. It is against us and in relationship to us, in part, that the client's conflict between Ego and Unconscious will be worked out. We represent "the other," that which proves to the client in concrete terms that his or her individual Ego is not everything and is not always in control. We must establish and maintain our own individual identity and, at the same time, support the client's identity, thus modeling the acceptance of differences.

After a great deal of effort at maintaining our own and supporting our client's individuality, at the appropriate moment we must be willing to change our focus. We must see that we are not only separate, each with our own personal story, but also part of the same myth or story. As a consequence of our relationship and the way our stories unfold, our growth is dependent on one another. Beyond this merging of personal myths, we soon begin to understand that we are both characters in a still larger myth, the evolutionary story of humankind. Each of us is transformed in the process of realizing the interconnectedness of all beings.

We have now added ourselves to the dreams, symbols, myths, and metaphors used by Jungians to access the deepest levels of the client's unconscious. Using a Jungian paradigm, we are a bridge from causality to teleology, from determinism to hope. We have moved away from the assumption that people are motivated solely by the gratification of self-centered impulses. We no longer resonate with the Freudian belief that "every individual is virtually an enemy of culture."[10] We believe that each of us possesses collective and social needs and a social conscience. Not only have we moved from biological motivators to cultural, but from cultural to spiritual. Jung says this trip from instinct to archetype is one of disparity at lower levels to the integrating tendency of commonalty and hope as it expands.[11]

Clients and therapists are now more like the quantum physicists who faced the particle and wave conflict until a new and transcendent understanding developed. We have moved from our existential loneliness into a relationship with the universe. The Jungian task of individuation, this move forward into relationship with the Unconscious, was anticipated by the Ego psychologists in their description of the progress of human development. They anticipated an identity crisis *marked* by the loneliness and alienation the client faced before visiting a Jungian therapist. They described a crisis of intimacy versus isolation, and the solution they suggested was relationship. Achieving intimacy, they told us, means giving up our usual autonomous position, allowing ourselves to be dependent and affiliate. The result of an inability to affiliate, they warned, is alienation and elitism. The position of the Ego is an alienated and lonely one. The Ego is autonomous; it stands alone. When the Ego relates to the greater whole, which Jung called the Collective Unconscious, it is no longer alone. In giving up power and control, we gain a meaningful place in the universe. "The orderly process of growth necessitates repeatedly letting go of the type of gratification and the urge to repeat it, in order to open one's Self to the new."[12]

The stages we have passed through from Freud to Jung are not nearly so neatly linear as I have implied, with one following on the heels of another. They overlap and repeat. Growth is more of a spiral than a line. We frequently circle back, approaching old stages from different vantage points. As the Ego gains new definition, we circle back to reorganize it, adding the material we are constantly retrieving from the personal unconscious. The Collective Unconscious is infinite, and our job of relating to it is never-ending. All relationships are always in process, demanding constant adjustment as they constantly change.

By now we realize that making boundary decisions from reason alone is dangerous. It leaves us unbalanced and too much in our heads. We also want to call upon a feminine way of knowing. This deeper wisdom, or intuition, is a knowing with the whole Self. It is not theory and cannot be analyzed or rationally explained. But this is not to imply that intuition is magical and ungrounded. There is a process people can go through to access their intuition and to become skillful in utilizing it. The first step in the process is simple acknowledgment that this is a valid way of knowing. Society has denied its legitimacy for centuries. Then we must begin to honor and respect it. When we respect our intuition, it will become more active and give us clearer messages. Next we need to study it and begin to understand what it actually is. Once we are more sure of what we are dealing with, we can cultivate it. We can test our intuitive powers. Allowing people to provide us with feedback, we can learn to recognize when our intuitions are accurate.

We as therapists actually do not reason out all the decisions we make. There is a level of communication and decision-making taking place that is not rational. It is intuitive. There is another source of information to help us make decisions about where our clients are in their developmental process and what kind of boundaries they need to have with us. We have been working from theory but also from intuition. Intuition is a kind of telepathy. It is contingent on merging boundaries with someone else, allowing us to know their experience as we know our own. It is the feminine way of knowing.

Defining this feminine way of knowing as intuition helps us to recognize it. Recognition and labeling is the first step toward losing our fear of intuition and developing it into a trusted skill. Remember what the quantum physicists discovered when they investigated the instant communication one photon miraculously had with the others. They discovered the only way to account for this instant communication was the understanding that the photons were not separate particles but interfused, connected. Just like these photons, therapists and their clients are interfused. We can intuitively know what each other thinks or needs because we are both a part of the big unified *us*. The Sufi master Pir Vilayat Inayat Khan repeats the words of Buddha when he first spoke after his years of meditation beneath the Bodhi tree. Buddha said that the word "me" no longer made sense to him.[13]

Our innate intuitive ability has a long history dating back to before the Goddess worshipers, the alchemists, and the Gnostics. Although given other labels, intuition has always been a part of the therapeutic tradition. It was recognized in what Freudians called transference and countertransference. In transference and countertransference, the client's and therapist's boundaries merge. They allow each other to hold or contain the disowned parts of themselves. This projection may be positive or negative but, in any case, the boundaries of client and therapist have merged and the disowned parts are felt as originating in the other person. You will recall that Robert Langs added a profound dimension to transference theory. He suggested that in addition to projected material, both the client and therapist know intuitively the wound of the other. What they do with the information depends on their relationship. Either they try to heal the other, or they use this information to have power over the other. Transference and countertransference are other names for a kind of intuition.

Intuition, this capacity to traverse boundaries, both excited and worried psychological theorists throughout history. They knew it had tremendous power which could be used both for healing and harm. Since Freud, there has been a movement away from separating and objectifying toward reciprocity and relationship. This was a movement from Logos to Eros, from rational to intuitive knowing. The humanists promoted Eros. Although they used it, they shied away from calling it intuition because they thought it sounded unscientific. Rogerian empathy was intuitive; however, it required merging with the client. Jung was the first to dare to publicly champion the feminine and an intuitive way of knowing. He even said the resurrection of Eros, the ability to interconnect, was society's only hope. Because of this, his theories were ostracized by many as mystic and unscientific.

When we therapists dare to break the scientific taboo and call intuition by its name, we have a valuable and powerful tool at our disposal. If we acknowledge with pride that we are mystics as well as scientists, we gain access to a tradition that has honored, respected, studied, explained, and exercised intuition for centuries. We can turn to the ancient and modern mystics as the experts they are and learn from them how to develop this time-honored skill.

There are many ways of developing intuition, but by far the oldest and most complete are the Eastern yogic practices. The Eastern yogics describe a developmental process similar to the one described by the Ego psychologists. In the beginning the yogis describe a state of participation mystique—no separate consciousness.

Slowly, they say, a primitive consciousness develops. At this early time, sensations rule and people's consciousness is like a raft tossed on the waves of phenomenal events. As people acquire the capacity to discriminate, they begin to have an "I," establishing their likes and dislikes, distinguishing between reality and fantasy. This discriminating "I" is equivalent to the Ego of Western psychology.

However, for the yogis this discriminative function we call Ego is not the final goal. They have a different objective: the gradual acceptance of more and more consciousness, eventually reaching unity consciousness. They see all other stages of development as steps toward this final goal. The goal is achieved by passing through an "I-It" consciousness and then merging to an "I-Thou" consciousness. Intuition is a product of an "I-Thou" unity of consciousness.

The yogic master has a similar job to the therapist. Neither therapists nor yogic masters can take their clients anywhere they have not been themselves. Both "must have a clear grasp of the traps and the pitfalls that lie along the road to self discovery and can bring a halt to the natural, joyful process of exploration and self discovery."[14] In order to develop intuition into a tool we can use, we therapists must learn to master it. We can do this by using the techniques of the Eastern mystics. Jungian theory has already transcended Ego and separateness. It began the expedition into the wilderness of the feminine. The yogis will now become our guides, providing the map and true compass our reticent voice needed. As our intuition becomes more familiar and safe, we will begin to feel comfortable about leaving the boundaries of our old role behind.

We want to become experts at determining the reliability of our intuitive judgment. To be as confident about using intuition as we are about theory, we need to turn our attention inward. The process of developing intuition is an internal journey. Recall the advice of the Roshi, "the entire world is the eyeball of a Buddhist monk...take one more step."[15]

The yogic traditions are rich and varied. They are each deserving of years of intense study and practice. Repetition and discipline are, as with every skill, necessary for mastery. But don't let this frighten or discourage you. Every step is movement in this process; it's enough to try. This is a journey of attitude and perspective, not facts and figures. There is nothing to memorize. The requirements are a Bodhi mind, humility, and openness.

The following are intuitive exercises chosen from various Eastern yogic traditions. There is a vast wealth of exercises available; even the few I present here are greatly abbreviated. These exercise are intended to give you a sample of and a feeling for the process of merging boundaries and developing intuition. They will launch you on an introspective journey which will explain the seeming paradox that to know yourself is to simultaneously know the other.

When presenting the use of Western psychological theory to make boundary decisions, I focused on assessing the client. In presenting these yogic exercises to develop intuition, I am speaking to the therapist. But in reality these are arbitrary choices. It is just as important for therapist to apply theory to self-assessment and for clients to work on developing their intuitive skill. And even this instruction is misguiding. We must remember that our separateness is an illusion.

As the experimenter cannot be separated from the experiment, the developmental process of the therapist cannot be separated from that of the client. So, put on your monk robe and take the first step.

Preparation

In preparation for the journey, remind yourself that your goal is to traverse boundaries and to know unity consciousness. You want to know yourself and the people you interact with as unlimited. The Sufi master Pir Vilayat Inayat Khan says that the journey you are about to take will help you "overcome [your] limitations in [your] understanding, in [your] circumstances, and in [your] relationships with people, and in [your] personality."[16] He recommends that to begin this internal journey, you must have an open and clear heart. In order to open your heart you must identify and then release your guilt and resentments. As helpful in achieving this goal, he suggests the following three exercises:[17]

1. Apologize for having done harm to others:

- Introspect honestly. Survey your most private feeling. Look for uneasy feelings caused by regrets, unpaid debts of any kind, bad advice given, times when you have hurt, used, or betrayed someone, or committed any kind of act which contradicts your values.

- Redress the wrong. Choosing the action that is most applicable for each situation, either ask forgiveness in your heart, take action such as apologizing or compensating the person, or make a gesture to society such as helping someone. Cleansing the conscience is a necessary part of opening the heart and awakening to unity consciousness.

2. Forgive others:

- Become aware of your wounds, such as being falsely accused or punished, being shamed or being betrayed.

- Avoid self-pity by either seeing the other's point of view or understanding how you have learned or grown from the situation. Letting go of attachment to resentment is part of opening the heart and awakening to unity consciousness.

3. Forgive the Deity:

- Focus on understanding the gain behind the loss. Try to see the "divine planning."

- See the difficult situation as a lesson causing you to face your fears and know you can do what you thought you couldn't. Through making suffering meaningful we open the heart and clear the way for awakening to unity consciousness.

Development of the Discriminative Function

This is the development of the small or the individual Ego of the Western tradition. In *Yoga and Psychother-*

apy, the authors tell us how the yogic traditions can help us gain freedom from our impulses, habits, and addictions. Instead of studying your external behaviors, as is the custom in Western psychological traditions, you will develop this discriminative function by observing your internal life. The following practices or exercises will help you mature from an identity that shifts from moment to moment to a more stable "I."

1. Quiet the body and mind:

- Begin by sitting in a comfortable position. Then track your awareness by saying, "Now I am aware of ____." Repeat the sentence each time as something new grabs your attention. For example, "Now I am aware my lips are dry. Now I am aware of the noise of the car driving by." Be the observer watching your sensations.

- Now focus on your breathing, taking full rhythmic breaths. Use your full lung capacity, inhaling and exhaling slowly, using your diaphragm and not just your chest and stomach muscles to help you breathe. Keeping your focus on your breath, notice the flow of mental events. Do not react to them, but as you notice your attention shifting, bring it back to the breath.

2. Find the observing "I":

- Be your own Roshi. Give yourself this koan: Who is the observing "I?" Who is it that is watching these sensations and thoughts go by? Who is it that was willing the breath, focusing on the breath, and willing the focus back to the breath when it was interrupted by other sensory awarenesses? Who is it that observes all of these levels at once? Think about these questions for several days. Who is asking these questions?

3. Use the observing "I" to discriminate:

- When you have identified this observing self within, begin to use it to make your decisions. As moment to moment decisions come up, turn within to this observing "I" and, accepting this as your identity, ask, Is this good for me? Do I want this? Do I like this? Make these decisions based on what is good for the observing "I." Do you notice a consistency developing?

4. Use the observing "I" to watch how you relate to your clients:

- When you are with a client, notice how you react. Do you like being the therapist? Do you like thinking of the client as a patient? Do you like being in the knowing position? Be completely honest with yourself about what you like and don't like about the interaction.

Moving Beyond Ego Identity

Remember, although it is a necessary part of the process, a stable Ego or "I" consciousness is not your final goal. Your next task is to enlarge your definition of Self, moving you closer to an identity that is more in tune with your potential, closer to Self-realization and unity consciousness.

1. Find the essence of the observing "I":

- Using an exercise from the Zen Buddhist tradition, look within, trying to discover what is the essence of the observing "I." Follow a path of deconstruction, taking off the layers of your identity one by one. Ask yourself this question, If I am not the roles I play (for example, mother, teacher, daughter, therapist) am I still me? Then do the same with your physical body, your emotions, and your thoughts. For example, ask, When my body ages and deteriorates, will I still be me? Am I essentially the same me when I am in a good mood or a bad mood, happy or sad? Am I essentially the same me when my opinions change? Find the big "I" that is more permanent and timeless, that doesn't change with the current views, social beliefs, and conditioning. Find the "I" that is not transitory. This is not the Ego "I"; it is a new, larger, eternal "I."

2. Practice not reinvesting in old patterns of behavior, in the habit[18]:

- Begin to use the eternal or big "I" to make evaluations and discriminations. Ask the eternal "I" to make the decisions you are confronted with during the day, including your behavior, feelings, and thoughts toward yourself and other people. When you have disidentified with sensory stimuli and the small "I" or Ego and are free from small thinking, habits and addictions, the Sufis say you are liberated.

Another method for accessing a boundariless unity[19]

1. See through the eyes of the Deity:

- The Sufis believe the world is a limited manifestation of the unlimited, and you are the eyes through which the Deity sees. Practice looking at the people and things around you as you imagine the Deity would. Think in terms of eons, not minutes. This is as large a perspective as you can have and still maintain duality.

2. Let go of the duality:

- Identify with the unity—no separate you, no separate Deity. Pir Vilayat Inayat Khan tells his disciples this is not a matter of will-power: "One's ego is shattered by the encounter with the meaningfulness or the greatness and beauty of life, God in life—a surrender to something greater than oneself."[20]

Having relationships that free and open you

Pir Vilayat also tells his disciples that relationships should make you more free to be yourself and more open to your possibilities. In order for this to occur, you must focus on the eternal form of the other and affirm their real beings. You must also be open to change. He suggests several exercises that will help you accomplish these goals in your relationships with clients.[21]

1. See the eternal qualities:

- Look at your client. Imagine what arche-typal or external qualities they embody (such things as love, power, beauty, cour-age, sexuality, wisdom, strength). Then ask yourself what you are doing in the relation-ship to support these qualities.

2. Be the witness:

- Imagine you are asked to be a witness on your clients' behalf. Focus on their identity beyond the phase they are in or their tem-porary condition. In your testimony relay to the court who they really are.

These practices are a beginning. With repetition they can help you improve your intuitive abilities. Through their use, you can develop the most important element to a healing relationship: a belief in the unlimited potential of human beings. Each time you practice these exercises, you will find it easier to break old habits and let go of old restrictions. Beyond the mo-mentary, separate identity, you will experience an eter-nal, interconnected whole.

Therapists can use both their theoretical knowledge and intuitive skills to provide the reticent voice with a good road map and true compass. We can feel a bit safer now to step out of our old therapeutic role into a truly reciprocal relationship with our clients. We don't have to know it all. Pioneering, even with a map and com-pass, will still be an adventure. What is required is our willingness to take the journey of the relationship. Thinking that we have to be perfect in order to proceed is a leftover belief from a time when the overextended perfectionistic masculine ruled. It is no longer relevant. Let it go!

"But somehow there is something one can do to begin, and then one unleashes a force that does it for him."[22] In order to begin the journey of relationship with clients, we must work hard on ourselves. We have to have "given up our attachments one by one, and expose [our] cherished fantasies to scrutiny...."[23] We must accept where we are in our own developmental process and the limitations of that stage of development. We then can ask ourselves whether we are ready to make the stretch necessary for change.

The boundary decisions we make with clients cannot be made alone. They must be made in reciprocity. We can share our knowledge and intuitions with our clients and then listen to theirs. We can teach them about the developmental process and get feedback about their needs and responses to us. We can ask our clients for their opinion and give them ours. This suggests a therapy premised on respect rather than domination, neither impotent nor coercive, but, as knowledge always is, inevitably empowering.[24] Therapists and clients are dependent on one another for success and growth. Personal involvement does not contaminate.

That is how we move together in this modern dance of relationship. We have transcended the contradictions of our old role: that of believing we know what is best for our clients and then expecting this unequal relationship to empower them. Our anxiety and confusion about taking on the new role was caused by our attachment to the old definition of the therapeutic relationship and our identification with the small "I."

In setting up a new dynamic reciprocity, we have created a therapeutic relationship which nurtures growth and personal power, one that will heal in our time.

> The arch of the moral universe is long but it
> bends toward Justice.[25]

VI.
ANECDOTES

Physicians say to me, "Well you're not talking statistics,...and you're telling stories, and they're all anecdotes and I say, "Wonderful. If an anecdote walks into your office don't kill them. Let them stay alive. Let them be an anecdote." They say, "Well that's a story." I say, "That's right. Maybe some day a story will walk into your office. Keep your eye out for one."[1]

Thus far this book is mostly history and theory supporting a kind of logical proof of its tenets. Although interesting enough in its own right, it is missing the interactional quality it promotes. The ideas in this book emerged and began to take shape out of my relationship with my clients. The solutions emerged from the interaction, the reciprocity. Each of us dared to reveal our needs in the therapeutic situation, and we were determined to persevere. So far I have not allowed the reader to be privy to this dialogue. As I finished, I realized that it was my clients who must write the last chapter.

I asked several of them, who were far along in their work with me and with whom I had periodically discussed the philosophy and purpose of the book, if they would be willing to share their experiences in therapy. I am indebted to them for the gifts they give by granting us permission to enter into their process. I applaud the courage and flexibility they demonstrated in risking a new kind of relationship with me in the midst of their deepest process.

When I transcribed the interview tapes, I was flattered but then grimaced as I thought their words seemed to glorify me. When I tried to edit out the references to me, I realized it was impossible. The process is truly one of relationship. It is always a dance in partnership, a joint undertaking. I believe that any therapist who is willing to be a partner in the dance of authentic relationship will receive similar answers from their clients.

The following are excerpts from these interviews. In the first set of interviews, I asked each client to answer two questions:

1. Looking back over the therapeutic work you have done, what was it that made therapy healing for you?

2. Now focusing your attention on the establishment of boundaries, how has a flexible approach to setting the boundaries between client and therapist affected you?

In the next set of interviews I asked clients who were also therapists to talk about healing and boundary decisions in both relationships. I asked them:

What about the therapeutic relationship was healing for you as a client, and how does this affect your work as a therapist?

In the last set of interviews I asked clients:

Where do you think you are in your developmental process, and how is the therapeutic relationship you are in affecting your progress?

I chose responses from these last set of interviews which exemplify three different developmental stages. The first describes the client's confusion and struggle to develop an Ego identity. The second illustrates the development of the discriminative function and the relaxation of the Super Ego. In the third the client is in the process of constellating the Self and feeling the elation of finding the meaning of life in relationship to the larger whole.

What Made Therapy Healing for You?

Jane

There was a time...I know exactly when it was. It was when you asked me about my hair. It was something one of my best friends would say to me. You said, "Have you ever thought about changing your hair back to its natural color?" And then it was like I knew that I could tell you just about anything. I could go with everything. If you remember, interestingly enough, that's when the memories really became...not just noticeable, but I couldn't avoid them any longer. And after that is when I started coming in and immediately curling up in the corner of the couch in the fetal position without even saying anything, because I knew that I could come here and I could do the work. So it is almost like when it went beyond a therapeutic approach, because, let's face it, "What are you going to do with your hair, or have you thought of dying your hair back" is not all that therapeutic. But I will never forget that.

It was like something my best friend would say to me...someone whom I trusted and felt comfortable enough with me to say that...to go beyond what seems to be the norm in therapy. You really personalized it. It told me that our relationship was, well...it felt like it was more than just, you know, you asking me questions and me answering them. Or more than just "uhm-uhm."

I mean I really don't think I could have done the work I've done, exposing or remembering something that I blocked for twenty years plus, with somebody who was just a therapist or just this professional that I saw once a week for an hour. There had to be more than that for me to really... I mean, you had to give me something to help me feel like I was going to be able to get through this and that I wasn't alone.

When you told me things like, "Well I'll call you tomorrow," well, you know one thing I know is that I have rarely heard of a psychologist or psychiatrist just calling their client to see how they are doing. In fact it is almost like they're not supposed to do that because it is not professional.

From someone who has been abused and who doesn't want to get hurt, and someone is getting close to you, at first you want to push them away. Okay. If you are pushing someone away they usually leave. But you never left. I never felt like you left...and even though I said, "No, No I'll be fine" or "You don't have to call me," there is a part of the child that was abused who really doesn't want to be alone. It takes time...I mean I had been in therapy for a year before I really called you.

I have been able to see how it's come full circle in the relationship to being healing in the sense that I, for the first time, could ask you, someone who I felt really cared, to come over and sit by me. You know, I needed it so bad at that moment and probably have needed it all my life, but never felt okay to ask for it. I wouldn't have felt okay if I felt like you were superior or if you were intimidating. I could never ask someone like that to come over and sit by me.

I have been in other therapeutic relationships, twice actually, where I didn't feel comfortable because...the one lady was a psychiatrist and she sat under this light and we had these chairs that swiveled but they were kind of hard. Hers was softer. And with the other one I was in a waiting room chair and he was in a big swivel, lean back chair. He always used to tell me what I needed to do. I knew that I couldn't do that and so I felt ashamed and I ended up, I mean I got worse...in both of these relationships I ended up getting worse. I never felt good enough. I always felt like the sick person, really sick.

Linda

I think it's real variable; it's not something that is always the same, depending where I'm at and where I come from in the process. I think that a good therapist knows that, can see that the client has gone to different levels and that they are evolving, or growing up. For me it feels like I have grown up a lot since I have been seeing you. And so I think that is one thing that is healing is knowing the client is changing, that I'm changing. And also it reminds me, too, of a parent-child relationship. Not like in the old days when we were growing up when the parents were the rulers and no matter what they said, we had to do it. Now kids speak up and we have to listen...I have to listen and I want to listen to my children. I think that's what happens here too; you listen, you are open to hearing that maybe I disagree and that I carry my own opinion.

It is also very similar to what we do in Twelve Step programs, where there is a sponsor and the sponsor's role, as I have learned to be one...some people sponsor the old way, but the most successful way that I have seen is that we are equal right from the beginning...one recovering person sharing with another. By sharing what we have been through, the other person maybe can admit they have done the same thing. If I know that you have been there, then maybe I might be more willing to say I have too. There is a lot of Ego and pride, sometimes I think it is really difficult or, it has been for me, to admit things, because I might feel that they are really horrible, that they are really bad things.

One of the first big healing things we talked about was my abortions. I really struggled with that a lot. I didn't feel any judgment from you at all, whereas in the past when I would try and work on that with other people, I did feel judged. I think it's really important that I am not being judged for something because I am doing it so much to myself that I can't bear to feel any more from anyone else. So that judgment, coming from that place of judgment that is not healing.

I saw a psychiatrist for a while and that was very weird. It was bad because of the drug therapy. I felt like I was being used as a guinea pig for all the different types of antidepressants, because it is a very hit-or-miss type of thing. I felt unsupported when I was doing really badly with certain antidepressants and I would call crying, feeling like I was going out of my mind. The voice on the other end of the phone didn't sound very nurturing. It sounded clinical, too clinical. "That's what happens when you take this kind of drug...a few days...give it a few days and see what happens. Call me back."

It made me feel very much "less than"...it really got me into this really strange relationship with the psychiatrist where I felt sort of like this bad little girl who would go and see her once a week. And she would sit in her chair doing her nails or falling asleep and I would be feeling more and more shame. It really hooked me into shame and I would go back every week for more and I felt like I couldn't live without her. She just didn't get it. So it made me feel stupid. Here is this psychiatrist with all these degrees and I am nobody, so I must be wrong. The old way of doing things, it makes the wound somehow bigger.

Then I went to another therapist before I came to see you. I saw her once and she was too easy. She said, "You are fine. You really don't need to see anybody." I knew I wasn't fine. I knew I had conned her. But when I saw you, you were not quick to jump on things...just to label me. You just said, "I'll see you next week, and write down your dreams so you can tell them to me." I caught on real fast that this was going to be a process...that it just wasn't something that I was going to come here for a little bit and you were going to fix it.

Rachel

Wow, well the first thing that comes to mind is getting support and having someone that understands me...supporting the ways that I think, the things that I want, even just the feelings that I have. Someone saying, "Yes that's okay. These are feelings that you have and they are legitimate." Not like what I have usually gotten, like "Oh, you are being silly," you know, or like, "You are just exaggerating" or something like that. Having you to say, "Yes it's okay. You are a real live human being and the things you feel are okay." Yes, support, encouraging me to do things, to take an active part in my life...improving it, changing it and growing.

I had a different experience with the therapist I had before, I mean, he was just, it felt like it was more his personal ego that was involved. Like he was going to go out and cure people and he was going to be solely responsible for it. Not help people but tell them exactly how to do it and what he thought they should do. I think he was very arrogant and not support-ive of me and a little belittling of me, negating the things that I had already done as not of any weight or value. He helped me feel the choices that I had already made were wrong and a waste of time. This is the same thing my family was telling me. I had a hard time with that as it was. I did not need him, who was supposed to be a professional, to depress me even more. Well, is that a therapeutic relationship? It is supposed to be but it is not. It is another abusive relationship.

He made me feel awful about myself. It's like he had a list of ABCD to be done. That was going to motivate me to be able to organize my life. In my case it was to organize my checkbook and to get my bills paid. Basically he was telling me that it was my fault these things were in a mess. That I just had to decide to do them.

What I later realized was that I was rebelling against what had been an abusive relationship in my childhood. It was one of the ways that I could, as an adult, make a choice to not do something. I mean I got stuck in that because I had no choice when I was little. Then I had to do it. So not doing my checkbook was a way of saying "No, No, No, No...I'm not going to."

What helped me to remember the abuse was learning that the things I think and feel and know are real. That I am not being silly or too sensitive, or exaggerating for dramatic effect. Yes, to believe myself, believe me. I am starting to find me, which is great. This makes me want to cry.

David

Well, your boundaries are different...or your willingness to cross personal boundaries is different from any therapist I have ever experienced. I am used to therapists setting ground rules when I walk in. Yes, I am yours for fifty minutes a week, but the rest of the time you are on your own. I guess somehow I am able to carry you with me in a little bag in my breast pocket, more than I have been able to with anyone else. It is not that I am just taking along so much the things you have told me. I have done role play with other therapists. "Dave, next time you are in such and such a situation, here is how to deal with it." I have been through all that and when I would try to do it it was phony and forced and I didn't have my heart behind it. It's the relationship with you and your sincerity that I carry around.

I feel I am part of your life not just part of your practice. I know because you have taken risks. When we got to the point of talking about personal feelings and you admitted that you found me attractive it meant so much to me. It was so personal and it made me lose so much of the shame that I had...the feeling that I was a totally unattractive person. Some kind of bridge was created that I have never before experienced. It's also because I knew that you took a chance. I know that therapists aren't supposed to admit a physical attraction. I guess that is probably the most important part. That you, someone who I really respect, thought I was worth something when, at that point, I certainly didn't think I was worth something. You might have left me out on a limb feeling shame...like it is stupid and hopeless for me to think someone would find me attractive because I am not worthy or attractive.

When I walk in for a session I kind of gear up like it's going to be some sort of intellectual joust. There have been times when I came in with my boundaries set and I have become just a scared little boy who just wants to rock back and forth in the corner...who just needs someone to sit there and hold his hand. You did. And God, that's probably not appropriate for a therapist. I mean I don't know...I just needed for someone to...I just needed physical contact.

Sometimes I need you to assert yourself as someone who knows something and can share it. Sometimes you have to say, "Dave, don't do that!" Give me the chance to decide whether it's legitimate for me instead of letting me always create my own truth. I have played that game for a long time and sometimes it doesn't work. It really gets nowhere. I know that fifteen years ago when I was engaged to this woman who was going to probably kill me with drugs and alcohol, I was with a therapist who was one of those guys who never said...who would never tell me what to do. Finally he said, "Dave, I've never told you what to do, but for once I am going to tell you what to do—don't marry her!" So I asked her to marry me the next week. But that was drugs and that time of my life. I hope that I have reached the maturity level where I am willing to do what someone else tells me to do. If I hear it and it's right for me, I will do it. It's not like it's coming from a parent.

Jody

I remember in the beginning that I didn't feel the formal part like a client going to a psychologist. It was more down to earth and that was what I needed. I never connected before...I didn't connect with my mother. I thought I connected with my dad but it wasn't the right kind of connecting. It was a really sick way of connecting. I wanted, I'm not consciously sure what I wanted, but I had a feeling for what I needed and sense of it and I went with my intuition.

Where I work I see psychologists who come in with little suits on and their collars buttoned up and they are very stiff and prim. I knew that wouldn't do me any good...it's not me. What I need was someone who was going to let me talk and who was going to listen to me and remember what I said. Something that was different from the way I grew up. Most of the time I didn't talk but even if I did it didn't matter. I needed someone to treat me like a real person, not a client or child. Someone I could connect with and build a relationship with.

I used to put people with degrees in a classification of "better than I am." Sometimes it is great for them to have these certificates and all that stuff, but sometimes even if they have them they are not the kind of person I need. That kind of formal attitude just heightens that feeling of me being less than, which is what I am in therapy to get over.

I need to do things without paying the high price of money and shame. I always felt that I had to pay to get my mother's attention. Several days after you and I went out together into the world, I had a strong image. I saw your car with my head raised next to yours and the feeling was, my mom cares enough about me to be seen with me. One of your roles is like a mom. As a child grows, their relationship with their mom should change. The child becomes more of a friend. They go out into the world together and do things more as equals. That's part of normal development. If you don't do this, the client or child stays a child. You have to see them as an adult.

I wonder when you as a therapist should be able to ask for your needs to be met in the relationship. If you don't then you keep the relationship on an uneven level. I am always the person in need, never the adult. That causes my self-esteem to be lower than yours.

About the Setting of Boundaries

Jane

I don't think setting boundaries was ever confusing because of the way you went about it. Whenever I said "no" you respected that. I remember times when you asked me if you could touch my shoulder when I was in a lot of pain or fear. I said "no," and you were fine with that. In fact you even helped me to practice saying "no." You just didn't push it. I think when someone invades your boundaries it's more about pushing. You just kind of presented it as an option. "I would be there for you in this way, if it's okay with you."

You allowed me to make the decision on my own, whereas a lot of times growing up I didn't have a choice, especially when I was being sexually abused I didn't have a choice.

If it is set up in a way that's not shaming, if it's okay to say "no"...I mean the fear is, well maybe my therapist won't like me if I don't do what he or she wants...you know, if it's set up so that the therapist likes you no matter what you do. It's like in Twelve Step programs...it's unconditional acceptance or love that creates a safe environment and that's always what I felt here.

It is more about getting close...it's about intimacy. If I didn't have that I would have never been able to work through all the feelings that I had or share those with you, or, you know, tell you things that were very difficult. How can you? I can't imagine. I haven't, for a long time, been able to get past getting honest with my history. I could tell people my history, but getting beyond that and getting into the feelings, it hasn't happened until now and I don't believe it would have happened without intimacy.

Linda

What we discovered the other day is that right now I think I still need to have a more traditional relationship with you. I need to continue the relationship as it is, it was never very traditional...but to keep it more where you are the psychologist and I am the client...and I can count on that stability. I think what we found out was that anything looser felt unstable for me and I felt like I suddenly was having too much responsibility. It was reminding me of my relationship with my mother and I don't want that.

Making these decisions about boundaries is hard. You have to pay attention to how it feels. It's a lot of work. It's not something like a script. It's not a script for me.

Rachel

Yes, well it's helped me to feel much more comfortable and relaxed knowing you are really concerned about me and my healing. That you are really involved and that this is not just a clinical study or a case...making it more personal. It is personal. It is me, it is my life. My other therapist was distant and impersonal. I felt used, like I was just another name on his roster, just another client to glorify his program.

I felt very close to you and that is more personal. I worry about overstepping my boundaries. I don't want to bug you too much or expect too much. But then the way we work, that would just be something I would bring up and we would talk about it. I am learning that I have the ability and the power to set boundaries. A lot of times I am afraid someone else is not going to be able to tell me, "Stop!" because I am just learning to do that. The other night I practiced with a friend. I wanted to talk about my latest abuse memory and I asked her if she could handle it and to tell me if she couldn't. It worked.

Another thing that helps in here is knowing I can change my mind. That is good to know because that is another part of my problem. Because I feel if I set a boundary then I have to stick with it. Otherwise I am wrong the first time. Now I can say that doesn't feel right any more. How nice. What a neat idea.

David

I now know that I have choices and I think I make better decisions about where to put the boundaries. I came in with this great need to open and reveal myself. I carried a hope that

I wouldn't get fucked in the process like I was as a kid. I wasn't taken advantage of here and because of that I think I make better choices about boundaries out in the world, dealing with people in business and program people. Sometimes I will just kind of stop and see that I set a boundary a lot closer to me than I normally would have. I feel powerful to be able to do that. And I am taking care of myself in the process.

Part of it is that I not longer see every situation as life-threatening, so therefore, it isn't imperative that I make the right decision on every issue. I can cut myself some slack. Sometimes I can make decisions frivolously and I never felt the freedom to do that before. Everything in my life was always life and death...making perfect decisions, saying the perfect thing. Now I can step on my tie every now and then. I guess you are going to ask me why, and it's because I can see myself as a little boy rocking in the corner.

I don't get the idea that you are going back to every psychology class you took to know how to deal with me. You are dealing with me in a loose kind of way. You give yourself an amount of leeway...you leave options open or allow yourself reactions that maybe a traditional therapist wouldn't, which allows me to do the same thing in my life. It teaches me to do the same thing in my life.

I see how you are in the world and I see your level of acceptance of who you are. I do kind of take that role for my own to some extent.

Maybe that is more important than anything you have to say. I am a believer that what we are says a lot more than what we say. Your attitude in the world, your attitude to the world is...you seem to wear it like a loose garment rather than a straitjacket and you don't seem to strangulate yourself the way I do.

Jody

I needed to do things with you outside of the office and I needed to be seen with you. I needed to learn how to interact with you in social situations simply like going to a restaurant and having lunch and overcoming the low self-esteem part connected with it and the anxiety and nervousness. My mother didn't do things like that with me and I felt that I wasn't good enough to be seen with her and that contributed to my low self-esteem. I needed to know that you weren't ashamed to be seen with me and that if I did something dumb it was okay...that your expectations were a lot less than mine. I hate to use the word normal because I don't know what that is and it really doesn't matter but, yours were a lot more relaxed than mine were.

Also, there was a particular workshop we both attended where it became really clear to me how deep the jealousy issue was for me. It happened because people didn't remember who I was. They forgot my name and that triggered all these old feelings. I tried to cover it up and I did okay until it was time...well it wasn't even time to leave...I chose to leave. I came up to you to say goodby and it was very apparent because I was very stiff and you knew I wasn't okay. I would have never talked about it had we not been together at that workshop...I probably wouldn't have said anything.

Then we had real live situations to deal with rather than working on it in the office. When we were outside the office this was spontaneous, it just happened. You could see my feelings and what happened to me...you could see better what I needed and how we could use therapy to help.

As a therapist myself...because of the particular situation I'm in, I'm faced with seeing some of my clients outside of the office too. I work in a chemical dependency treatment center with the after-care population. I stress to them, as a part of their program, that they need to go to meetings, work the steps, and that they need to reach out and get people to help them. Being in the program myself, I have the same needs. It puts me in conflict if I don't go with my heart open. At meetings everyone is someone just like me, working on recovery. I think it would be harmful to them and to me for me to say like, "I can't talk with you because you are a client." That's not life.

It makes sense to do it this way...to put ourselves in the position of having to decide where the boundaries are and when they need to be here and when they need to be there...because that's what life is all about.

What better way is there to learn how to make these decisions as part of therapy but in a live situation rather than sit in the office and talk about it? When something happens we can go back and talk about it. We talk about how we feel, we talk about what needs to change. We share what's going on. It's not like following a book and an outline in black and white—you have to do it this way...no matter what happens...you can't live that way.

It's great to know that if either of us wanted something from the other we would talk about it...that's what would happen. And we would work through it. If you said we couldn't do something I would have a couple of feelings. If it was because of the law I would be real angry at the law for not keeping up with life. I would be angry that we reached a point in therapy, which we spent a lot of time and a lot of feelings to get to, and then we would have to stop because the law says you can't go any further. If it was because you didn't want to, if it was not right for you, I might initially be hurt but then I would be proud of you for standing up for your needs. I also believe that is something we need to learn how to handle. That is part of growing.

Sometimes I believe I have offered too much to my clients. I think I have gotten a lot better in the last several year. Some of that is through my therapy with you. Being able to stand up for myself and say this is not what I need, I have to take some time for me. With other clients I learned to back off because I knew my needs were getting in the way and that it could be harmful and I wasn't going to let that happen.

It's helped me with my relationships in my family as well. My expectations are much more realistic and mature. A burden has been lifted. We're also working on boundary issues together. I'm testing boundaries with you and applying them to other relationships.

I want to say something more and I don't know how this is going to come out. Because mostly I am a nonverbal person and I would rather draw a picture and I am also an intro-vert...so I am feeling very tearful. It is because talking about all this is stirring up a lot of feelings about what we have done together and how much it means to me. I can say how much it means to us. I know that this rela-tionship is meaningful to you too. I can feel that today. I know that by the way you act, by the things you say and do. Because of your vulnerability, because of the way you show me that it's meaningful to you. When some-thing happens and I see a tear in your eye. I know that I mean something to you, that I matter. And it's not just a tear of empathy. No, no it's different, I have seen that tear too. It's not that tear.

What About the Therapeutic Relationship Was Healing for You as a Client, and How Did This Affect Your Work as a Therapist?

Marian

I can speak a little as a client and then as a therapist...which is pretty cool because it is hard to think that as a therapist I am supposed to know everything and as a patient I am supposed to know nothing when I am the same person. I love it. It sort of shows up the system for what it is.

You are open but genuine; not new age-y. I would not do well with a trendy sort of thing. That wouldn't work for me. It would feel kind of phony...'cause it seems like with that kind of stuff there are no boundaries. There have to be some boundaries. I have to feel like I am here for me. I want to say, "How are you?" but then I want to have the luxury of saying I want to talk about me.

My growth has to do with a spiritual thing. It's a respect for parts of me that are more feeling and less head. What I feel is that you are able to respect; like I said, you can honor the parts of me that have been really hard for me to nurture.

I think that is what it is about healing. What it is for the kids I work with. I have such a hard time. I squelch the kids because I have been squelched. When they start to show that part of themselves, instead of being able to accept it, I probably get as scared as my parents got when I was trying to be whoever I was.

That makes me think about being a therapist. Here I am being a therapist all day. There is the question of what it is I am supposed to be doing. Part of what I come up against is my formal training. It is really hard because my inclination is to have fewer boundaries and to give my clients more of myself. Because to me a relationship is a circular thing. They give to me and I give to them. I get into a struggle about that. I have one particular client it is most like that with. She told me about Stain Stick, how good it was. That was great. She brought me a coupon for it. There was something about that that was sort of circular and it feels right.

I just want to be human with them. This is how I ended the day today with an eleven year old that bounces; who just avoids, avoids, avoids talking about or really even dealing with the big issues in her life. I just said, "Carley, we both know that there are big things going on. I am here to help you but I can't make you talk about these things." I can't. In that way it feels human to just say it and I like it. When I don't put so much pressure on myself to cure them right away, to change them, to make them better...

Well, I think it has to do with that whole thing of being taught all these theories. Trying to follow the theory gets exhausting. It is really stifling when my mind starts doing that. It is mixed up with Ego and intellectualizing the process... It is not helpful because then my Ego is kicked up and I start thinking about the therapist down the hall. She would really be able to set some boundaries here. The kid is running out of my office or something. There is a judgment from inside and outside. The judgment is that I am not doing a good job. I am not helping. Then I lose my ability to be with them, really be with them. It is clear with me, yes, when I am just able to be with them and not worry about theory, good things happen.

It sounds like I know a lot of what has been healing for me but when I go to be a therapist I get all mixed up in judging myself and what I have been taught and others judging me and lose myself. Accepting would be good. Not using the words "appropriate" and "inappropriate" so much, you know. As a client what heals me is learning to trust and respect myself. Yes, and that is what would be healing for them too. So I should trust and respect them, or else do the same thing to them everyone else has.

It is just so tough. There are a lot of rules we have been taught. They say what you can and cannot do with clients. I think that limits the healing with some clients. Especially with the kids. Sometimes they need to be touched. I mean I have never been able to just hold a child. That is not allowed at my agency. There is all this stuff around sex. There are times when holding is what they need. They need intimacy. They need to feel safe in an intimate relationship. Yes, and we are prohibited. It is sad.

Mary

What comes to mind for me is not being judged and to feel that there is mutual value...that I would be valued by you...that it matters to you that I am all right. Also that there is a sense of involvement in the process, both yours as the therapist and mine as the client. There must be a sharing of the therapist's process as well as the client's.

I think there is more danger in not knowing the therapist's process than in knowing it. What interfered for me with past therapists was wondering how they could have no reaction. What kind of person is that? I mean it's not human. There is no warmth. It just doesn't seem real to have someone not react or respond to me. I think it is harmful.

There must be a balance to it too. There are times when there needs to be a distance...so there has to be an ability to come in and out of, or to change the distance...of knowing when it is okay. As a therapist I look to my own process when I make these decisions. I listen to my own feeling, in my body, my heart. I really trust what it is saying to me, when it is okay to reach out or when it is better not to. Like touching a client, or leaving them alone. Like leaving my chair and sitting with them, or staying put. They are really clear messages to me.

And I listen to my clients too. I might say,
"This is what I'm feeling. What would you like
to do?" I would check it out before I made an
adjustment in the role or in the boundary.
Also it depends on their history and all that.
I would use all the skill that I have as a
therapist to make the best judgment including information from myself and from my
client.

One of the things that is really healing about
any relationship, and that includes the therapeutic relationship, is that the communication is ongoing. Changes in power or role are
talked about. It is all part of the relationship
so it is all discussed. It is all a piece of the
growth on both sides. I think that's all a part
of relationship.

As a therapist you do have specific skills, but
that is something I bring into a relationship
with me whether it is a therapeutic relationship or a love relationship or a business relationship. That is something that is a part of
me. In terms of responsibility I am responsible in the sense of being in the world and
being with people. I am responsible for how I
am with people, any people. So that piece of
the question does not change. There is a
difference in role, but in some sense, that is
more a mechanical difference than a difference in essence. There are certain requirements of me when I sit in the therapeutic
chair that are dictated by the role and the
office. But I think, in essence, what makes it
healing is that sense of genuineness coming
from me that is beyond the role...that is, that

I value them or connect with them on a level of relationship that is not dictated by the role. It is about who I am as a human being and how I want to be with you. What is healing is a connection beyond the role. If the client perceives that from me, then it is a healing relationship.

I don't like the idea that there is only one place in the world where I could speak to my clients or with my therapist. I want to be a real person. That's what I am and I don't want to take on roles and attitudes that aren't possible for me to live up to. I am not god-like, you know. Demystifying does not make therapy less potent; not for me. It makes it lose some of its fear. For me to think that a client is less than a therapist is to be a hypocrite...because I am a client as well as a therapist.

Really there is a change coming in the culture anyway toward a much more healing way of being with each other in the world. Therapy is relationship...it's in a different setting but it's the same game everywhere. The same stakes. I have a lot of respect, or I try to have a lot of respect for people everywhere. The more I learn about what happens in the therapeutic relationship and how fragile and wounded many people are, the more careful I am in the world...because people aren't different. I can cause as much destruction at Revco as I can in my office.

Where Do You Think You Are in Your Developmental Process, and How Is the Therapeutic Relationship You Are in Affecting Your Progress?

Gail, on the struggle to develop an Ego identity

Well, we've come to understand that I get lost in my unconscious life. My life is like my dreams where I'm asking questions. I have things that I look up to, like these symbols, and I come to them and I ask what they mean. But I get lost in there and know I need a clearer feeling about myself and that I feel so lost.

My life is feeling more real than it used to, but I'm so busy being in it that I don't have time to look around me and be like, "Wow, who is really doing all of this?" I mean therapy feels like doing that. And that's what makes me feel real. So I can look at it from the outside.

Um, in therapy I get to look at myself existing. And I see what I am like in this medium that is life. I'm very existing. I'm not existing because of the things that are around me, the people that are around me, not defined by the outside, I'm there, I'm real.

It is good to have that ability to look at the motions, look at me being in motion. Because if I look at what's going by instead of looking at the inside, which is what I always do, I'm lost. I would say you're a still point. Like

you're a thing that I can go by and see as I'm
going by it. But I realize in the past year, that
that's not true. Because you're moving too.
It's just that you're moving in a way I understand or something. That makes me cry; because it's good.

If you move settings, if you move surround-
ings, then I'll be distracted for a while and
then I'll think about it, "How am I existing in
this place?" But then eventually I will forget
that because it's not important. What's important is just the connection from a place
that's beyond all the changes.

Our relationship has perspective that I can
just be in. That is different from all other
perspectives I have. Okay, the way it feels
when I'm talking with you is like the difference between water and ice. I mean ice is
water, but it's solid. You think it's solid, but
it's not because you can see through it. So if
you spend all your time thinking about the
properties, you will finally realize what it really is. You just have to realize that it is.

If I was in my lost place in the world when I
was here with you, I wouldn't be able to talk
about it. I have to be out of it too. I think the
thing that helps me with getting an identity
the most is having someone listen to me
saying what I want and then seeing that I'm
not doing it. Then I know that I know what I
want, but I'm just not doing it. Because I can
talk myself out of listening to myself. But
you're listening to me, you know what I'm
saying and you say it back to me when we talk

about it, and eventually I know what I really want and I do it. Just reminding me that I have my own convictions helps.

Elanore, on the development of the discriminative function and the relaxation of the Super Ego

It seems like I'm developing more of an Ego. It's not the critical one that says something has to be perfect or has to be right, but it's more of the one that says take time out, look at all the alternatives, look at the variables, and do what's best for you. And it takes time to do that. And to be comfortable and relaxed with that. It doesn't have to feel like, "Gratify this instantly," like, "I want this. Grab it!" That's who I was. Chasing around. Now I'm more of a calm person who can say, I don't have to do this right away, I don't have to put it off either. There's a choice. You can work with the alternatives and do what's good for you. Because that's important to you. It's very different, thinking in terms of what's good for you instead of what's perfect. Well, either Id was the driver saying, "I want this, I want that, I need this, I need that," or this Super Ego slave master saying, "You shouldn't have this, you shouldn't have that."

A lot of what's helped with that here, I think, is your objectivity in showing me what I do and how I think. It's not like my relationship with my friend Shelly where I would say, "I'm a crummy person for doing that," and she would say, "No you're not." What you say is,

"Gee, that's really tough on yourself." "Are you sure you want to be that tough on yourself?" is what's implied in what you say. Your doing that over a period of time has kind of brought me up short and made me think, do I really want to be that tough on myself? You don't give me a chance to do what I do with Shelly. What I would do is come back and say, "Yes I am," And we get into this, "No you're not!" "Yes I am!"

That's part of it. And the other part is that I think that you care and you believe in me and see things. You have a vision for me. You relate to who I really am under the critical layers. I think I've already had some knowing it was there too, that it's always been. Nobody else has seen that in my life. My family certainly doesn't. There is absolutely no one in my family who sees that.

Kim, on the process of constellating the Self and feeling the elation of finding the meaning of her life in relationship to the larger whole

I just have such a sense of trusting that it's satisfying to say there is something larger than me. There is finally meaning and there is sort of a method to the madness of my life. And I don't fully understand it.

There is something hopeful about seeing beyond, or seeing the big picture of what I really am. I never had that. I just kept trying to please others. I kept trying to put things on myself. There is a wonderful part of a book I just read about somebody who sort of tries on personalities, like Sears fashions. I kept doing that. I would just keep trying different costumes. I would collect them, searching for the right one, the right fit. And now, finally, what I'm doing fits. I think I'm just flooded with this absolute sense of clarity and peace and hope and purpose. I mean it's like there is a reason for me existing, and it's not just to make my family miserable. And it frees me so much. I mean it's indescribable the difference between those moments and all the others.

What has helped with that here, what comes to mind is that word, "mutual." You know, I don't feel power struggles with you, I have a very clear sense that you are the therapist. I am so thankful that you are the therapist and yet, I think it's part of what my whole sense of what this sort of therapy is about. It's this whole sense that you really can do it differently, therapy and life. You can do, I can do, what we believe in. And you can't necessarily define it the way we've been taught, but it's real, it's helping me to become who I really am.

For me it's about respect and validation that go so hand in hand. And a lot of what I struggled with with my last therapist was because she saw our roles in such a set way. So much of what she did just fed right into my feeling invalidated that I had to put on another Sears costume for her. There are a couple of things we've done here that have helped me to dare to see the meaning of my life in this big sense. There are the dreams we've worked on. I know you know that there is more to me than the little me here trying on Sears costumes. And then there's our relationship. I have the absolute sense that you take care of yourself and you do your own work on yourself, that you are or have been in therapy. That is a big thing to me because of my mother's neurotic stuff. That's an important thing you can do as a therapist is to take care of yourself and own your own stuff.

And then there is daring to have therapy this way that's validating for me. Because nobody does it this way. Everyone says it's wrong to be personal and that it can't be done, and you have to have these rigid boundaries and you can't meet people as equals and as people. Then I have an idea about myself. I think I just have had this idea but I didn't see it because everyone said I should be some other way or some other thing. And what happens with you makes me know that that's not true. That it is possible. It really can be done. I think it's pretty amazing.

Endnotes

Introduction

1. Richard Wilhelm, *The I Ching or The Book of Changes*, third translation, trans. Cary F. Baynes (Princeton, New Jersey: Princeton University Press, 1969), lvi.

2. Department of Professional Regulation, Board of Professional Examiners, *Rules of the Department of Professional Regulation Board of Psychological Examiners* chapter 21V-15.004 (Tallahassee, Florida: Department of Professional Regulation, 1987), 9.

3. Merle A. Fossum and Marilyn I. Mason, *Facing Shame* (New York and London: W. W. Norton and Co., 1986), 164.

I. History

1. Wilhelm, *The I Ching*, 300.

2. Lawrence Frank, "Freud and Dora: Blindness and Insight" in *Seduction and Theory*, ed. Dianne Hunter (Ubana and Chicago: University of Illinois Press, 1989).

3. Martin Buber, *I and Thou*, trans. Ronald Gregor Smith (New York: Collier Books, 1958).

4. Edward C. Whitmont, *The Symbolic Quest: Basic Concepts of Analytical Psychology* (Princeton, New Jersey: Princeton University Press, 1969), 268.

5. Erich Neuman, "On the Moon and Matriarchal Consciousness," in *Fathers and Mothers: Five Papers on the Archetypal Background of Family Psychology*, by Erich Neuman, Augusto Vitale, Muray Stein, James Hillman and Vera VonderHeydt (Zurich: Spring Publication, 1973), 43.

6. Vocatta George, *The History of the Goddess and the Transpersonal Significance of her Decline and Re-emergence in the West* (Ann Arbor, Michigan: University Microfilms, 1986), 7.

7. Neuman, "On The Moon," 47.

8. Ibid., 58.

9. George, *History of the Goddess*, 67, 77.

10. Thomas Bulfinch, *Bulfinch's Mythology* (New York: Thomas Y. Crowell, 1970), 1-11.

11. George, *History of the Goddess*, 104.

12. Neuman, "On the Moon," 40-63.

13. *The Holy Bible: Old and New Testament in the King James version* (USA: Random House, 1943, A. S. Barns and Co. Inc., Publishers of the Modern Library), 961.

14. Neuman, "On the Moon," 40-63.

15. Emma Jung and Marie-Louise Von Franz, *The Grail Legend*, trans. Andrea Dykes (Boston: SYGO Press, 1970), 379-399.

16. George, *History of the Goddess*.

17. Elaine Pagels, *The Gnostic Gospels* (New York: Vintage Books and Random House, 1981), 38.

18. Ibid., xix.

19. Ibid., 12-13.

20. Ibid., 13.

21. Ibid., 15.

22. George, *History of the Goddess*, 138, citing Jim Robinson, ed., *The Nag Hamadi Library*, (Netherlands: E. J. Brill and Harper and Row, 1977), 165.

23. George, *History of the Goddess*, iv.

24. Pagels, *Gnostic Gospels*, 57.

25. George, *History of the Goddess*, 113, citing Exodus 34:11-14).

26. Ibid., 9.

27. Ibid., 9.

28. Pagels, *Gnostic Gospels*, 15-16.

29. Barbara Ehrenreich and Deirdre English, *Complaints and Disorders: The Sexual Politics of Sickness* (New York: The Feminist Press at the University of New York, 1973), 6-7.

30. George, *History of the Goddess*, 150, citing R. R. Ruether, *Religion and Sexism—Images of Women in the Jewish and Christian tradition* (New York: Simon and Schuster, 1974), 105.

31. Pagels, *Gnostic Gospels*, 74, citing I Corinthians.

32. Ibid., 76, citing I Clement 1.3.

33. Camille B. Wortman and Elizabeth F. Loftus, *Psychology* (New York: Alfred A Knopf, 1988), 251.

34. Carol Gilligan, *In A Different Voice: Psychological Theory and Women's Development* (Cambridge, Massachusetts: Harvard University Press, 1982).

II. Science

1. Wilhelm, *The I Ching*, 271.

2. Evelyn Fox Keller, *Reflections on Gender and Science* (New Haven and London: Yale University Press, 1985), 6-7.

3. Ibid., 53-54.

4. Ibid., 52.

5. Ibid.

6. Edward F. Edinger, *Anatomy of the Psyche: Alchemical Symbolism in Psychotherapy* (La Salle, Illinois: Open Court, 1988), 4-9.

7. Ibid., 9.

8. Ibid., 3.

9. Keller, *Reflections*, 52.

10. Ibid., 64.

11. Buber, *I and Thou*, 11.

12. Keller, *Reflections*, 54.

13. Ibid., 12.

14. Ibid.

15. Ibid., 53.

16. Ibid., 72.

17. Casey Meller and Kate Swift, *The Handbook of Nonsexist Writing* (New York: Harper and Row, 1988), 4.

18. Gary Zukov, *The Dancing Wu Li Masters: an overview of the new physics* (Bungay, Suffolk, Great Britian: The Chaucer Press, 1979), 50.

19. Ibid., 50.

20. Ibid.

21. Ibid.

22. Ibid., 48.

23. Ibid.

24. Ibid., 44.

25. Ibid., 87.

26. Stephen Addiss, *The Art Of Zen* (New York: Henry N. Abrams, Inc., 1989), 107.

27. Ibid.

28. Zukov, *Dancing Wu Li Masters*, 133.

29. Addiss, *Art Of Zen*, 107.

30. Keller, *Reflections*, 132.

31. Ibid., 159.

32. Ibid., 171.

33. Buber, *I and Thou*, 11.

34. Keller, *Reflections*, 11.

35. Ibid., 134-135.

III. Therapy

1. Wilhelm, *The I Ching*, 287.

2. Michael Fouchalt, *The History of Sexuality, Volume 1: An Introduction* (New York: Vantage Books, 1980), 59.

2. Ibid.

3. Ibid., 64.

4. Ibid., 71.

5. Keller, *Reflections*, 101.

6. Ibid., 95-114.

7. Ibid.

8. Ibid., 106.

9. Ibid., 86, citing Hans Leowald, "The Waning of the Oedipus Complex," *Journal of the American Psychoanalytic Association* 27, no. 4, 751-75.

10. Keller, *Reflections*, 95-114.

11. Martha Noel Evans, "Hysteria and the Seduction of Theory" in *Seduction and Theory*, ed. Dianne Hunter (Urbana and Chicago: University of Illinois Press, 1989).

12. Charlotte Perkins Gilman, *The Yellow Wallpaper* (Old Westbury New York: The Feminist Press, 1973), 24.

13. Frank, "Freud and Dora," 127, citing James Strachey et al, ed. and trans., *The Complete Psychological Works of Sigmond Freud* (London: Hogarth Press, 1953-74), 216.

14. Evans, "Hysteria," *Seduction*, 79.

15. Frank, "Freud and Dora," 119, citing Strachey et al., *Psychological Works*, 216.

16. Bruno Bettelheim, *Freud and Man's Soul* (New York: Vintage Books, a division of Random House, 1984).

17. Robert Langs, *A Comprehensive Course in Psychoanalytic Psychotherapy: Psychotherapy Tape Library* (New York: Jason Aronson Press Inc.), tape 1.

18. Ibid., tape 1.

19. Robert Langs, *The Therapeutic Interaction Volume 2: A Critical Overview and Syntheses* (New York: Jason Aronson, Inc., 1976), 578.

20. Zukov, *Dancing Wu Li Masters*, 73.

21. Langs, *Therapeutic Interaction 2*, 577.

22. Ibid., 582-83.

23. Langs, *Comprehensive Course in Psychoanalytic Psychotherapy*, tape 7.

24. Ibid., tape 3.

IV. The Next Step

1. Wilhelm, *The I Ching*, 281-2.

2. Keller, *Reflections*, 104.

3. Sheldon Kopp, *Back To One: A Practical Guide for Psychotherapists* (Palo Alto: Science and Behavior Books, Inc., 1977), 3.

4. Ibid., 130.

5. Ibid.

6. Keller, *Reflections*, 140.

7. Adolf Guggenbuhl-Craig, *Power in the Helping Professions* (Dallas: Spring Publications, Inc., 1971), 154.

8. Ibid., 124.

9. Ibid., 135.

10. Ibid., 155.

11. Ibid., 135.

12. Ibid.

13. Wilhelm, *The I Ching*, 300.

V. Setting Boundaries

1. Pir Vilayat Inayat Khan, *The Retreat Manual Part 1,* ed. Paran Khan Bair and Lakshmi Barta Norton, unpublished guide for carrying on a spiritual retreat (Lebanon Springs, New York: Sufi Order Publications, 1980), 2.

2. Marija Gimbutas, *The World of the Goddess*, a presentation on tape (Fairfax, California: The Green Earth Foundation, 1990).

3. Swami Rama, Rudolph Ballentine, M.D., and Swami Ajaja, Ph.D., *Yoga and Psychotherapy: The Evolution of Consciousness* (Honesdale, Pennsylvania: The Himalayan International Institute of Yoga Science and Philosophy, 1976), 182.

4. Edward C. Whitmont, *The Symbolic Quest: Basic Concepts of Analytical Psychology* (Princeton: Princeton University Press, 1969), 249.

5. Calvin S. Hall and Gardner Lindzey, eds. *Theories of Personality,* third edition (New York, Chicago, Bisbane, Toronto, Singapore: John Wiley and Sons, 1957), 280, citing Carl Rogers, *On Becoming a Person* (Boston: Houghton Mifflin, 1961), 185.

6. Ibid.

7. Ibid., 290, citing Carl Rogers, *Client Centered Therapy; its current practice, implications, and theory* (Boston: Houghton Mifflin, 1951), 517.

8. Ibid., 120, citing C. G. Jung, "The Psychology of the Unconscious" in *Collected Works* vol. 13 (Princeton: Princeton University Press, 1953), 114.

9. Whitmont, *Symbolic Quest*, 83.

10. Swami Rama, Ballentine, M.D., and Swami Ajaja, Ph.D., *Yoga and Psychotherapy*, 97.

11. Ibid., 125.

12. Ibid., 179.

13. Khan, *Retreat Manual*, 32.

14. Swami Rama, Ballentine, M.D., and Swami Ajaja, Ph.D., *Yoga and Psychotherapy*, 175.

15. Addiss, *Art Of Zen*, 107.

16. Khan, *Retreat Manual*, 6.

17. Ibid, 1-10.

18. Swami Rama, Ballentine, M.D., and Swami Ajaja, Ph.D., *Yoga and Psychotherapy*, chapter 5, 64-104.

19. Khan, *Retreat Manual*, Introduction.

20. Ibid., 18.

21. Ibid., c.1-c.6.

22. Ibid., 4.

23. Swami Rama, Ballentine, M.D., and Swami Ajaja, Ph.D., *Yoga and Psychotherapy*, 201.

24. Keller, *Reflections*, 134-135.

25. Taylor Branch, *Parting The Waters: America in the King Years, 1954-1963*, quoting the abolutionist preacher Theodore Parker (New York: Simon and Schuster, 1988), 197.

VI. Anecdotes

1. Bernie S. Siegel, M.D., *Life, Hope and Healing* (Chicago: Nightengale Conant Corporation, 1988), audiocassette.

Index

Get in Touch with Your Core Energies

WHISPERS OF THE HEART: A Journey Toward Befriending Yourself

Dale R. Olen

Paperbound, $8.95
180 pages, 5½ x 8½
ISBN 0-89390-100-8

The author's central message is that behavior arises from core energies that are good: the energy to exist, the energy to act freely, the energy to love. The diagram below illustrates how these energies figure in the psychological journey to your heart. This practical book will help you relate more effectively with others and enter more fully into your daily life experiences.

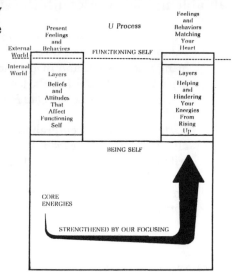

Order from your local bookseller, or use the order form on the last page.

Resources for Grief Ministry

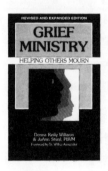

GRIEF MINISTRY:
Helping Others Mourn
Revised Edition

*Donna Reilly Williams
& JoAnn Sturzl*

Paperbound, $14.95
195 pages, 5½ x 8½
ISBN 0-89390-233-0

Grief Ministry: Helping Others Mourn has been revised and expanded to include new chapters on AIDS and job-related grief experiences. This is an indispensable guide for anyone helping another through any type of loss. Educators, clergy, healthcare professionals, and pastoral ministers will find this book invaluable in their work with the sick and bereaved.

> "A wonderfully sensitive, compassionate, well-balanced overview of a complex subject that will bring information and inspiration to the grief experience." — Rabbi Dr. Earl A. Grollman, author of *Living When a Loved One Has Died*

> "*Grief Ministry* is comprehensive, while additionally detailed and focused. It will make a real contribution to the field of death and dying." — Linda E. Harper, Bereavement Coordinator, Kaiser Permanente Hospice Program, Norwalk, California

Order from your local bookseller, or use the order form on the last page.

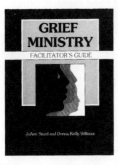

GRIEF MINISTRY FACILITATOR'S GUIDE

*JoAnn Sturzl &
Donna Reilly Williams*

Paperbound, $19.95
144 perforated pages, 8½" x 11"
ISBN 0-89390-228-4

This new grief ministry training guide shows you how to set up a program using the authors' *Grief Ministry: Helping Others Mourn Revised Edition* as a textbook. Everything you need to successfully train grief ministers to serve the bereaved in your community is included: listening and roleplaying exercises, discussion topics, meditations, a guest speaker preparation sheet, scripture readings, resource listings, and plenty of useful handouts with photocopy permission included.

> "Anyone involved in the preparation of lay persons for pastoral visiting or bereavement support will be encouraged by the *Grief Ministry Facilitator's Guide.* The experiential nature of the program leaves both facilitator and participant spiritually enriched, theologically grounded, personally affirmed, engaged in their own healing, and equipped with valuable insights into the mourning process." — Mamie Dawson, Chaplain, Grey Nuns Hospital, Edmonton, Alberta

Order from your local bookseller, or use the order form on the last page.

Improve Your Group Facilitation Skills!

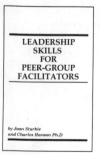

LEADERSHIP SKILLS FOR PEER GROUP FACILITATORS

*Joan Sturkie &
Charles Hanson, Ph.D.*

Paperbound, $11.95
144 pages, 5½" x 8½"
ISBN 0-89390-232-2

This handy guidebook will help you brush up on group leadership skills. Some areas of focus are inclusion, active listening, openness, and empowerment. The authors also address common problems in group situations and offer ways to resolve them.

— — — — — — — — — — — — —

Order Form

Order from your local bookseller, or mail this form to Resource Publications, Inc., 160 E. Virginia St., #290, San Jose, CA 95112-5876, (408) 286-8505, FAX (408) 287-8748.

Qty.	Title	Price	Total
___	_____	___	___
___	_____	___	___
___	_____	___	___
___	_____	___	___

Subtotal ____
CA residents add 7¼% sales tax
(8¼% in Santa Clara County) ____
Postage & handling
($2 for orders up to $20;
10% of order for orders over
$20 but less than $150;
$15 for orders of $150 or more.) ____
Total amount enclosed ____

☐ My check/purchase order is enclosed.

☐ Charge my ☐ VISA ☐ MC.

Expiration Date _____

Card # _____-_____-_____-_____

Signature_____

Name _____

Institution_____

Street _____

C/S/Z_____

PI